Psychic Abilities

Successful Dating Secrets

Single and Alone No More!

Know Yourself and Find Your Perfect Partner. Improve Your Love Life and Build a Happy, Healthy Relationship.

John K. Hunt

© **Copyright 2022 - All rights reserved.**

The content contained within this book may not be reproduced, duplicated or transmitted without direct written permission from the author or the publisher.

Under no circumstances will any blame or legal responsibility be held against the publisher, or author, for any damages, reparation, or monetary loss due to the information contained within this book, either directly or indirectly.

Legal Notice:

This book is copyright protected. It is only for personal use. You cannot amend, distribute, sell, use, quote or paraphrase any part, or the content within this book, without the consent of the author or publisher.

Disclaimer Notice:

Please note the information contained within this document is for educational and entertainment purposes only. All effort has been executed to present accurate, up to date, reliable, complete information. No warranties of any kind are declared or implied. Readers acknowledge that the author is not engaged in the rendering of legal, financial, medical or professional advice. The content within this book has been derived from various sources. Please consult a licensed professional before attempting any techniques outlined in this book.

By reading this document, the reader agrees that under no circumstances is the author responsible for any losses, direct or indirect, that are incurred as a result of the use of the information contained within this document, including, but not limited to, errors, omissions, or inaccuracies.

Meet John K. Hunt

John K. Hunt is an author, consultant, active philanthropist, and a strong advocate for mental health.

He is the author of *"Empath & Psychic Abilities - Successful Dating Secrets"*, and in this book, he draws upon his own experiences with dating while applying empath and psychic abilities to help singles achieve better results.

He is known for his innovative approach to dating and relationships, which has received much attention in recent years. He has developed unique exercises and techniques to help people tap into their innermost selves and unlock their full potential in their quest for love.

John is an expert on dating and relationships. Having spent over 10 years helping people find love using empathy and psychic abilities, he shares his wealth of knowledge in his writing. Not to mention, he's used them himself! He knows how to combine these skills with traditional dating advice to give singles the best chance of finding their soulmate. He believes that finding true love is a difficult task. However, with the right mindset and skillset, anyone can find their way to their soul mate and build a healthy relationship with them.

As a philanthropist, he has partnered with several organizations that promote healthy relationships and support those struggling with emotional challenges. John also contributes to causes such as education, poverty alleviation, and environmental protection. He believes that a better world begins with better relationships and is committed to making a positive difference in all aspects of society.

In addition to his work as an author and dating and relationship consultant, John K. Hunt is known for his commitment to personal growth and self-improvement. He believes that people must first focus on becoming the best version of themselves to attract healthy relationships. This concept is central to his teachings, and he frequently emphasizes the importance of personal growth and self-discovery in his writings.

John's desire to help others stems from his own past struggles with relationships and mental health. He overcame his own obstacles to become an expert in his field and uses his experiences and insights to help others do the same.

With his unique combination of personal experience, psychic abilities, and practical advice, John K. Hunt is poised to continue making a significant impact in the world of dating, relationships, and mental health. He is a true inspiration to many, and his unwavering commitment to helping others discover the best version of themselves, love, and happiness is a testament to his passion and dedication.

John is a credible source, especially when it comes to relationships and dating, and his advice is sure to help anyone looking for love. So, if you're ready to find love and take your dating skills to the next level, you can learn more about John's techniques and advice in this book.

Table of Contents

INTRODUCTION 11

CHAPTER 1: YOUR LOVE LIFE 13

WHAT DOES LOVE MEAN TO YOU? 13
YOUR DREAM PARTNER 15
   Know More About Yourself 16
   Consider Core Values and Characteristics 17
   Imagine Your Dream Relationship 19
   Be Realistic 19
HOW TO HAVE THE LOVE LIFE YOU DESIRE 20
   The Dating Mindset 20
   Having a Positive Attitude 22

CHAPTER 2: THE ART OF SEDUCTION 25

THE ROLE OF SEDUCTION FOR DATING 25
   You Attract What You Desire 26
   Screening Possible Partners 27
   Maintaining a Power Balance 28
HOW TO MASTER SEDUCTION 28
   Steps to Follow 29
   Some Rules of Seduction 30
WHAT NOT TO DO 33

CHAPTER 3: CONFIDENCE IS KEY 35

THE IMPORTANCE OF CONFIDENCE FOR DATING 35
   Improving Your Relationships 36
   You Choose the Right Relationships 37
   Improving Your Sex Life 38
BEGINNERS' NERVES 39
   Stay Present in the Moment 39
   Practice Makes Perfect 41
HOW TO BUILD DATING CONFIDENCE 42
   Create a Pre-Date Routine 42
   Consider How Great You Are as a Date 44

Prepare Questions *45*
Don't Put So Much Pressure on Yourself *47*

CHAPTER 4: LOVE HYPNOSIS AND TELEPATHY 51

USING HYPNOTHERAPY FOR YOUR LOVE LIFE 51
HOW IT WORKS 53
THINGS YOU SHOULD KNOW 54
HOW TO PRACTICE TELEPATHY 55

CHAPTER 5: IMPROVE YOUR SEX LIFE 57

WORKING ON INTIMACY 57
How Intimate Are You? *57*
How to Be More Intimate *60*
THE IMPORTANCE OF A HEALTHY SEX LIFE 63
HOW TO IMPROVE YOUR SEX LIFE 64
Improving Your Sex Life While Single *65*
Have a Conversation With Your Partner *66*
Improve Your Fitness *68*
Be Adventurous *68*
Don't Do Anything You Wouldn't Be Comfortable With *70*

CHAPTER 6: HOW TO FIND THE RIGHT PARTNER 71

KNOW WHAT YOU'RE LOOKING FOR 71
Have High Standards *72*
Reconsider Your Dream Partner *72*
Consider Common Interests and Values *73*
General Things to Look For *74*
Don't Limit Yourself Too Much *76*
CONSIDER YOUR COMPATIBILITY 76
Do You Click? *77*
PUTTING YOURSELF OUT THERE 78
Try Dating Apps *78*
Shoot Your Shot *79*
Make the First Move *80*
Ask Your Friends to Set You Up *81*
Be Open to Opportunities *82*
Avoid the Toxic Ones *84*

CHAPTER 7: BUILDING HEALTHY RELATIONSHIPS 85

THE IMPORTANCE OF HEALTHY RELATIONSHIPS 85
Having a Comfortable Relationship *86*

How to Have a Healthy Relationship 87
How to Improve Yourself 87
   Be Your Own Individual *88*
   Work on Self-Love *91*
   Self-Improvement Activity *93*
Managing Conflict 95
   You and Your Partner Against the Issue *95*
   Stay Calm *96*

CHAPTER 8: AVOID RED FLAGS 99

What Are Red Flags? 99
How to Notice Red Flags 101
   Analyzing People *103*
Do You Have Red Flags? 104
   How to Determine if You Have Red Flags *104*
Activities to Avoid Red Flags 108
   The Toxic Checklist - Avoiding Red Flags in Others *108*
   Journaling Activity - Eliminating Your Red Flags *110*

CHAPTER 9: IMPROVING COMMUNICATION SKILLS 113

The Impact of Communication on Your Love Life 113
How to Be a Better Communicator on Dates 115
   Utilize Small Talk *115*
   Conversation Starters *116*
   Ask Questions *118*
   Utilizing Effective Body Language *118*
   How to Read Body Language *120*
   Communication Don'ts *121*
   Examples of Effective Dating Communication *123*
How to Be a Better Communicator in a Relationship 126
   Be Open and Honest *126*
   Listening to Your Partner *128*
   Couple Communication Exercises *129*

CHAPTER 10: LEARNING EMOTIONAL INTELLIGENCE 135

The Importance of Emotional Intelligence in Love 135
Have You Found "The One"? 136
   Consider Your Feelings *137*
   How Your Life Has Been Impacted *138*
   What You Need vs What You Want *139*
Understanding Intuition 141

How to Enhance Your Intuition 142
HOW TO BE MORE EMOTIONALLY INTELLIGENT 143
　Activity 1 - The Four Rs 143
　Activity 2 - Identifying Your Emotions 145
　Activity 3 - Responding Over Reacting 146
WHAT TO DO IF YOUR PARTNER HAS LOW EMOTIONAL INTELLIGENCE 147

CONCLUSION **149**

A MESSAGE FROM THE AUTHOR **151**

Introduction

You're tired of your dull dating life that seems to be going nowhere in your life. Your average night is you sitting in front of the television alone, eating crappy food, and wishing your life had more thrill with a companion by your side. Introducing dating to your life can provide you with ample thrills and happiness, which will leave you feeling content.

If you've been out of the dating game for a while, you may struggle to get back into the swing of things. You no longer know how to successfully date and you're unsure of how to get people to like you. This makes dating a daunting and overwhelming experience, when it should actually be enjoyable and fun.

This book will help you to approach dating with a more confident and positive attitude. You will be able to put all of your nerves, worries, and reasons for anxiety to the side because you will be able to focus on the positive aspects of dating. Although nobody can have a perfect dating life, as you will experience uncomfortable dates, rejection, and awkward moments, it's important to appreciate each experience in the moment.

Whatever you want from your dating life, this book will teach you how to retrieve it. If you're looking to date casually, improve your sex life, or have some fun short-term relationships, you can learn how to fulfill this lifestyle in a healthy way. On the other hand, if you want a long-term healthy relationship that provides you with comfort, this book can teach you how to approach dating in order to find "the one."

Knowing what you want from your love life before you get out there will help you to make the most of dating. You will feel fulfilled and attract the right individual with your seductive skills and love hypnosis. Utilizing the art of seduction can help you to attract the partner you desire, while hypnotherapy will help you to become the potential partner that attracts "the one" for you.

Chapter 1:

Your Love Life

Whether we like to admit it or not, we all need a love life that makes us feel happy and satisfied. We all long for a life partner who will make us feel more complete in life, so it's important for you to ensure that the romantic aspect of your life is prioritized. It can be easy to get carried away by your personal or professional life, which causes you to ignore your love life. However, life is all about balance, so it's crucial that you don't overlook your dating life.

Through this chapter, you will learn more about your love life and what you're looking for. In order to discover how to seek the love and affection you desire, you need to learn about what you want from your love life. This information will help you to understand what you need to do to transform your dating life in the way you desire.

What Does Love Mean to You?

Everyone has a different idea of love and why it's so important. Even if it's not something you think about often, love means something personal to you. It's important for you to answer the following question before you pursue a dating life.: "What does love mean to you?". This is the ultimate question that we all have to ask ourselves at some point in life.

You need to understand what love means to you so that you can pursue a dating life that will bring you fulfillment and genuine happiness. With this question, you can ask yourself a set of follow-up questions that can help you to understand what love means to you. These are a few questions you can explore:

- *What is my love language?* There are five different love languages which include acts of service, words of affirmation, physical touch, receiving gifts, and quality time. We all have a love language that we prioritize more than the others. You may have never considered which love language you prefer, but we each have a preference that's important in our relationships. When you get into a relationship, it's important to voice the type of love language you need.

- *How do I express love?* When you're thinking about love languages, you should also consider how you express love to others. You may prefer words of affirmation and verbal romantic expression, but you express love in a more physical manner. Consider the difference between how you express love and what you expect to receive from your partner. How you express love naturally can give you a look at what love means to you.

- *What type of love do I admire?* We've all watched a movie, witnessed a cute couple, or read a romantic book where we admired the love people or characters experience. For some, seeing romantic, lovey-dovey affection makes them wish they were in that type of relationship; or when they see a couple acting like best friends and laughing together, it makes them desire such a comfortable relationship. The type of love you admire watching is usually the type of love that you wish for yourself.

Love could mean so many different things to you; the best way to discover its meaning is by discovering what type of love makes you feel best. Whether you're a more physically affectionate person or someone who loves to hear sweet words, love does mean something valuable to you. The core of love is what brings us together, as it gives us the same satisfying and fulfilling feeling. Once you know what type of love and expression gives you this feeling, you can have success as you pursue dating.

Your Dream Partner

When you're discovering what you want from your romantic life, understanding what you want from a partner is important. Most of us have a checklist for the perfect partner that we want, and it's important that the right person checks all of the boxes. Although it's important to have an idea of what you need and want from a partner, it's also important to remember not to restrict yourself. The perfect partner for you may not be someone you expected, but rather someone you needed.

With that being said, it's still valuable to take the time to consider who your dream partner would be. You need to look for someone who has the right characteristics, morals, ideas, and passions as you. It's these aspects of an individual that can make your relationship more successful. So, take some time to consider what your idea of the perfect partner is. These are just a few ways you can find a partner who aligns with you perfectly and enhances your quality of life.

Know More About Yourself

Before considering who your dream partner may be, you need to know and understand who you are first. This may sound ridiculous to you, as you probably think you know everything there is to know about yourself. The funny thing is, many of us go through life unaware of our true essence and what makes us the individuals we are. A few things you should consider about yourself before you get into a relationship include the following:

- **Your morals.** Start off by asking yourself what your morals and values are. You need to consider the values that you carry close to your heart, as they make an impact on the type of partner you need. Your values make up your core personality, so you need to date individuals with the same morals and values as you. If you date someone with different morals and values, you may find yourself compromising your beliefs to relate to them.

- **Your interests.** Another thing you should consider when you're trying to know yourself better are your interests in life. You may be someone who believes you're not interested in much, but if you take time to look at what makes you happy in life, you will find that you have interests that make up a big part of your life. Ultimately, you'll want a partner who shares similar interests as you do because this will help you to connect and bond with each other.

- **Your weaknesses.** Not only should you look at the positive aspects of yourself, but you must also take the time to consider your negatives. Unfortunately, none of us are perfect, so we need to be able to address our weaknesses before pursuing dating. When you learn about the negative side of yourself, it can actually help you to find the right partner for yourself. You need to find someone who will love and accept your flaws, as well as help you to become the best version of yourself.

Learning more about yourself can ultimately help you discover what you want and need from a partner. You need to take time to discover more about yourself so that you can find someone suitable for you. Knowing more about yourself can also help you determine what you need and should expect from a relationship.

Consider Core Values and Characteristics

Once you've learned more about yourself and what you want from a partner, it's important to consider the values and characteristics you would like your potential partner to uphold. What aspects of an individual's personality and values are important for you in a relationship?

How people behave, think, act, as well as what they value most in their lives can have a drastic impact on any relationship. This is why it's so important to consider all of these factors when you're dating. You want to discover what aspects of an individual are valuable to you and any romantic relationship you want to pursue. These are a few things you can look for in a person that aligns with your idea of a dream partner:

- **Humanitarian values.** You may want to find a partner who cares deeply about others. You find it important to spread kindness and care about other people around you, so you expect your romantic partner to hold the same values as you. This is something you can look for in a partner so that you can be with someone who cares about people as much as you do. If this is something important to you, you should look for a partner who displays genuine empathy and spreads kindness and love to others.

- **Outgoing personality.** You may be searching for someone with a more outgoing personality, as this is a big preference for you. If you're a more reserved individual, you may need an outgoing person to balance you; or if you're already an outgoing person, you may only find yourself attracted to people who are as outgoing as you are. How your partner reacts around you and others is crucial, as you may prefer to have a more outgoing or introverted partner.

- **A sense of humor.** To many people, having a sense of humor is a make-or-break quality for a relationship. Everyone has different personalities, and if you're a jokester then you'll need someone who shares your sense of humor. There are also different types of senses of humor that you can have. You may want someone to have a cynical sense of humor like you, or someone who can relate to your dad's jokes. Being able to have someone to share a laugh with every day is important.

- **Confidence without cockiness.** For most of us, confidence can be a very attractive trait. When someone has pure confidence in themselves, it helps you to view them in a positive light. However, just because you want someone confident, doesn't mean you want someone cocky. This is why it's important to be specific about the characteristics you desire from your future partner. Ensure that you look for someone both humble and confident, instead of someone who rubs their cockiness in your face.

Imagine Your Dream Relationship

When you're thinking of who your dream partner may be, you should take some time to imagine your dream relationship. When you envision the lifestyle you want to live with your dream partner, it helps you to realize what you're looking for in a significant other. Try to imagine yourself in the type of relationship that you've always dreamed of.

Take some time to yourself to imagine the type of relationship and lifestyle you desire to live with your partner. You may want to live a life of traveling around the world and going on exciting adventures, which means you need a partner who shares these same interests. Or, you could want a stable and secure future, with children and financial security, which means you need to seek a partner who is on the right path in life.

By imagining the life you want to live with your dream partner, you make yourself aware of what's required of them. You realize what makes them important to you and what type of person would be most suitable in your life. Knowing this will allow you to find a partner who has the same objectives and dreams as you, which will allow you to live fulfilling and loving lives together.

Be Realistic

Lastly, you need to be able to have a sense of realism when you're considering who your dream partner could be. When we say your "perfect" partner, it doesn't mean that this person must be literally perfect, because that is impossible. This merely means that you must find a partner who is perfectly suited to you. The perfect partner is still a human being with flaws, weaknesses, and the ability to make mistakes. Their negatives actually make them more lovable for you, as their strengths and positive characteristics make them perfect in your eyes.

Although this dream partner has everything you desire, you need to be realistic by understanding that they have a negative side to them—everyone does. So, when you're looking for a partner, you must ensure that you're lenient with your desires. The person you may click with might not tick all the boxes, but this doesn't mean that they aren't a great catch.

It's all about having a balance of healthy standards and realistic expectations. This will help you to seek the perfect partner who makes you happy. Yes, they will have their flaws and they may not be the exact type of partner you've dreamed of, but they will be suitable for you if you look for them with an open mind.

How to Have the Love Life You Desire

Now that you know more about yourself and what you want from a potential partner and your love life, it's important to consider how you will turn your love life into what you desire. Throughout this book, you will learn how to achieve the dating life that brings you real happiness. Before you learn how to make this your reality, you need to discover how to have the right mindset and attitude to attract the love life you desire.

The Dating Mindset

If you want to get into the dating world and successfully transform your love life, you need to develop a healthy dating mindset. Your mentality will influence how you behave on dates, the people you connect with, and how much you enjoy your dating life.

It's valuable to adjust your mindset before embarking on dates, as this will help you to approach each date with a fresh perspective.

- **Have an open mind.** When you're exploring different options as you date, you need to be able to have an open mind. Although you may have a vision of the perfect partner and perfect relationship you want for yourself, you need to be open minded when you meet new people. You never know what type of person will become the perfect partner for you. You also may experience dates that aren't as enjoyable and successful, but this doesn't mean they were a waste of time. These types of dates can be seen as a form of experience that helps you become a more confident dater.

- **Do what makes you comfortable.** Yes, it is important to have an open mind when dating people, but this doesn't mean you should continue a date you're not happy or comfortable with. Often as people pleasers, it can be easy to get yourself sucked into a relationship you don't want to be in. You become too scared to tell the other person you're not interested, or that you're stuck in a position you're not happy with. This is why you should have the mindset of prioritizing yourself and your happiness. You're allowed to say no to a second date and turn someone down if you're not interested.

- **Have a motive for your dating life.** Going on date after date can be draining, even when you do take the necessary breaks. You may start feeling unmotivated to pursue dating anymore because you're tired of experiencing rejection, bad dates, and the anxiety of putting yourself out there. You want to quit pursuing your love life because you think it's hopeless. If you're dating a lot, you're bound to experience a rough patch like this. For moments like this, it's crucial to keep your eye on the prize. You need to have a motive that pushes you to continue your romantic journey. This motive may be because you're lonely and you really need a partner or just to meet new people. Reminding yourself of this motive will get you past all the negative experiences.

- **Don't overthink.** Ultimately, the best way to make dating a pleasant experience for you is by avoiding overthinking by all costs. When you begin to overthink before a date, by telling yourself you're going to mess up and it's not going to be good, this is when dating becomes less enjoyable. Dating really isn't the scariest thing to do, so don't convince your mind that it's the worst task. At the end of the day, it's important to realize that responsible dating can't harm you in any way, no matter how nervous you are. So, just go for it and make the most of each experience!

Having a Positive Attitude

Your attitude toward dating will ultimately result in how enjoyable your dating experience is for you. If you view dates as something daunting that you dread happening, you will never make the connections you want. You need to have an optimistic and positive attitude toward dating, as this will help you to make the most of each dating experience.

The attitude you have toward a date influences how well it goes. Believe it or not, the person you date will be able to sense whether you want to be on that date with them or not. If you want to create a real bond with someone, you need to show them that you're excited and happy to get to know them, which can easily be achieved with a positive attitude.

At the end of the day, your attitude toward dating will attract the type of experience you have. This entire dating journey is in your control, so why not feel positive and excited about it? Enjoy the ride, the different experiences, and the benefits of improving your love life. You must practice patience, as it may take time for you to find the one, but this doesn't mean it's impossible!

Chapter 2:

The Art of Seduction

When it comes to dating, understanding the art of seduction is crucial. Being able to practice seduction as you date helps you to have the upper hand. Utilizing seduction gives you a sense of power, which can be used to persuade romantic partners. With the power of seduction, responsibility must come. However, if you choose to use the information in this chapter, ensure that you use the power of seduction to positively influence your relationships.

The Role of Seduction for Dating

Many people have a very negative view of seduction, as they think it's a form of manipulation that is harmful to others. However, seduction can actually be an effective way to attract the love life you desire. It is true that seduction can be negative when it's used incorrectly with wrong intentions, but this doesn't mean that it can't provide you with healthy benefits in your dating life.

The key is to know how to use seduction in a positive and healthy way, which is what you'll learn through this chapter. When you master seduction, you will find that it benefits your love life in numerous ways. These are just a few benefits you can experience from making the most of seduction throughout your dating journey.

You Attract What You Desire

The main reason why seduction is so effective when dating is because you attract what you desire from your love life. You have an idea of what you want from a partner, and when you find someone who ticks all the boxes for you, you're able to captivate them in your trance. Being able to use seduction with individuals you're interested in dating will give you a better chance at winning them over. You can attract what you desire from your love life in the following ways:

- **Captivating a crush's attention.** Through the art of seduction, you're able to tempt, mesmerize, and attract attention by using all the tips and rules you will learn throughout this chapter. When you use your seductive skills, you're able to intrigue anyone you're interested in. You may be thinking that your crush is way out of your league, but you'll be surprised to find out how interested they are in you when you show them how desirable you can be.

- **Keeping potential partners interested.** Not only can you captivate the attention of someone you're interested in, but you can also use your seductive skills to keep people around. We've all experienced relationships where it's exciting in the beginning, but it doesn't take long for it to fizzle out, which can cause you to leave the other person. When you're seductive, you're able to maintain the interest of the people you date, as they always want to see where the relationship will go next.

- **Develop relationships.** With the use of seduction, you have the power to elevate a relationship. You may find that you are more in control of the relationship than the other partner, which means you can get exactly what you want from the relationship. If you want to have a more serious long-term relationship, you can attract someone who wants that and convince them that you're the right partner for them.

Believe it or not, you have the power to attract the partner and love you desire in your life. We can often believe that love happens to us, but we don't take into consideration that we have a lot of control in the situation. Using seduction helps you to find control in your love life, as you're able to attract what you want.

Screening Possible Partners

Using seduction can also help you see things with more clarity. You discover what the motives are of the people you date when you use seduction, which helps you to steer clear of the individuals with the wrong intentions. This will help you to hold onto the right partners who fill you with happiness.

For example, if you're using your seduction to attract a person you like, and your intention is to look for a long-term committed relationship, you may find that their intentions are just to have sexual relations and a casual relationship. When you're using seduction to attract them, they become forceful to engage in sexual activities with you, instead of making the effort to get to know you.

You can discover a lot by attracting the dates you want to like. You may find that they're looking for something long-term, when you want to have something casual and fun. Or, you may even find a gold digger, who is adamant about knowing how much money you have and whether you'll spend it all on them or not. Use this information wisely so that you can continue seducing a partner with intentions that align with what you desire.

Maintaining a Power Balance

Whether we like to admit it or not, all relationships have one person who is more powerful or dominant than the other person. If you're currently in a relationship, think to yourself—who wears the pants? I know this may seem like an outdated statement because everyone is seen as equal these days. However, there are some power and control differences in every relationship.

When you master the art of seduction, you will find that you possess a bit more power than your partner does. This doesn't mean that you rule them or undermine them, it just means that you can call more of the shots and your opinion is usually valued highly. If you find yourself having more power in a relationship, you need to nurture this power responsibly.

You can use this power and control to make your relationship better and healthier, instead of using it to manipulate it into what you want. If you use this power to assert dominance over the person you're dating, you're bound to scare them off. Nobody wants to feel like they are controlled by someone, so you need to know your limits and boundaries.

How to Master Seduction

You may think that you're not a seductive individual, but everyone has this side of themselves, whether it's obvious or more hidden. It's all about tapping into this side of yourself so that you can fully embrace the art of seduction. You're able to use seduction to transform your dating life, you just need to believe in yourself and your ability to utilize the following steps and rules.

Steps to Follow

If you're trying to master the art of seduction, you're going to want to follow a step-by-step guide that gets you into the mindset of being seductive. Seduction may come easily to you, but if it doesn't, these steps will help you to find the confidence and ability to be a more seductive individual. Try out the following steps if you're getting started with seduction:

1. **Relax.** Before you begin following any practical steps for seduction, you need to be able to relax and calm down. People who successfully seduce others have a sense of confidence, belonging, and assertiveness that can only be accomplished when they're relaxed and calm. You won't be convincing in your seduction if you seem worried, nervous, or uncomfortable. Before you start, ensure that you're calm and ready to embrace the next steps.

2. **Be independent and distant.** You may be really enthusiastic about practicing seduction, but you mustn't let this excitement cause you to appear desperate. You need to avoid being needy and over the top, as this can be a major deterrent for anyone you date. You need to master the art of being casual, distant, and independent. Do things such as ghosting the person you're talking to, be unavailable at times, and be nonchalant.

3. **Utilize effective body language.** When people think of being seductive, they usually focus on the words they say and their actions. This can cause you to forget about the importance of effective body language. You can use your

body language to flirt with and seduce the person you're dating or pursuing. Your eyes specifically have a seductive power which can be embraced through strong eye contact, flirty looks, and winks. You can also flirt through contact by gently touching the person you're talking to, as well as getting close to them. There's so much you can say with your body that you may find challenging to say with seductive words.

4. **Be playful.** Being seductive is not only about being serious and assertive, as this can become very monotonous and boring. When you're being seductive, you also need to be playful and flirtatious so that you can captivate the attention of the person you're pursuing. Being more playful can actually make you more attractive and alluring to others. You can achieve this by touching, teasing, and flirting in a casual and playful manner. You want to appear as someone who is fun with a good sense of humor.

5. **Be patient.** Lastly, it's important for you to remain patient. You may follow all these steps and do everything you can, but you still don't get the results you wished for. Or, you may find that you try to be seductive by using these steps but it doesn't occur naturally for you. Being a seductive individual takes time and practice, so be patient with yourself. Over time, you will find yourself naturally being seductive and attracting the type of relationships you want.

Some Rules of Seduction

If you want to learn how to seduce dates, it's important to understand the various rules of seduction that make it so effective. Although the art of seduction can be subjective to each individual, there are rules in place to ensure that it's managed successfully. These are merely a few rules of seduction that you must respect and follow on your dating journey:

- **Become tempting.** If you want to draw someone you're interested in closer to you, you need to appear tempting to them. You need to catch their attention somehow, as this will make them intrigued to pursue you. You can create temptation by giving the other person a glimpse of the potential pleasures to come. This will show them that you have something desirable to offer them, which intrigues them and piques their curiosity. Ensure that you are vague with your temptation, as you want to leave room for mystery.

- **Keep them on their toes.** Once you have successfully captivated the attention of someone, you need to find ways to maintain their interest. The best way to accomplish this is by keeping them on their toes. You don't want to appear too eager and forward, as this will get rid of any mystery or intrigue. By keeping them in suspense for what's to come next, they will feel more captivated and intrigued enough to stick around because they want to see how things unfold with you.

- **Mix pleasure with pain.** You may want to appear kind and charming at first, but being too nice won't get you anywhere with seduction. If you want to use seduction, your objective is not to make the other person feel safe and secure in your relationship. When you're continuously nice and safe for them, it ends up becoming monotonous. If you'd like to continue to keep an individual on their toes, you must do things to keep them guessing. For example, give them space without telling them so that they can wonder why you've distanced yourself. This will make them feel more attached to you, as they want your attention back.

- **Be vulnerable.** Although being dominant, strong, and assertive is important for seduction, you can't keep this act going forever. With this persona, you also need to have moments where you appear more vulnerable and weak. If you look too rough and strategic, it may make the other individual think you're someone to avoid. This is why it's important to showcase your weaknesses and vulnerabilities to show that you're only human as well. This will make the other person feel sympathetic toward you, and you can end up turning their sympathy into love. Don't be afraid to make your partner feel stronger through your vulnerability, as this can do wonders for your relationship.

- **Beware of what's to come.** Once you've mastered seduction and have learned how to captivate your targets, it's important to be prepared for the aftermath. Seduction is extremely powerful, so you may find yourself being overwhelmed by the results of your craft. Unfortunately, successfully practicing seduction can come with negative side effects. You may find that it doesn't provide a secure, healthy foundation for a long-term relationship, so be careful of how you use it.

Although there are rules for seduction, you shouldn't let this limit you. Seduction can actually be seen as an art form that you're in control of, so why not improvise and make the most of it?

The major key for success in seduction is having confidence. If you are confident and assertive with your words and actions, you'll be able to seduce others easily.

What Not to Do

As you've probably gathered by now, there is a negative side to using seduction. If it's not practiced responsibility, it can be toxic and hurtful to potential partners or dates. This is why it's important to learn how to prevent yourself from using the dark side of seduction. Here are some don'ts that you should try to avoid by all means:

- **Do not use seduction to deceive others.** Although seduction is used to benefit you, it should not be used to deceive people into being with you in any way. At the end of the day, you need to live through honesty and integrity, because lying and deceiving may work in the short-term, but it will bite you in the butt in the long-term. You can't force anyone to love you and you shouldn't lie about who you are to attract others.

- **Do not use seduction to hurt others.** If you use seduction with ill intentions, you can end up hurting the people you date. You may find that you do or say things that truly offend others. With seduction, you need to avoid being harmful or offensive to others. Don't say manipulative words and participate in guilt tripping or bullying, as this will only negatively impact your relationship with this person.

- **Do not use seduction for sexual manipulation.** One of the major no-nos you must respect is not using seduction to sexually manipulate others. You cannot use your seduction skills to manipulate romantic partners into doing things sexually, especially if it's something they're not comfortable with. If someone you're dating doesn't want to engage in sexual activity with you, you have to respect them and make them feel comfortable no matter what. Manipulating them into doing it will only hurt them and create a very toxic relationship.

At the end of the day, you have the power to make your seductive abilities positive or negative. If you want to have a healthy, positive experience in your dating life then you need to be able to explore the good side of seduction. You can reap the benefits of seduction in your life by keeping other people on their toes and being mysterious and desirable.

Chapter 3:

Confidence Is Key

If you're trying to get into the dating scene, having confidence is key. When you're shy and reserved in the dating world, you'll find yourself struggling to make an impact. Sometimes you need to be able to make the first move when you're dating so that you can make a good first impression. Just as much as dating may make you nervous, it makes other people feel just as scared.

When you take that first step with another, it breaks the awkwardness and silence between you both, which ultimately allows you to get closer to them. Having confidence can help you create meaningful relationships and enter the dating world with a bang. You may not think you'll be successful at dating, which breaks your confidence; however, everyone has the ability to be good at dating.

The Importance of Confidence for Dating

You need to be able to have confidence within yourself before you start pursuing romantic relationships with other people. You can't love and care for other people if you don't have love and care for yourself. Having confidence when you date can also help you to be more successful in your love life. You will find that it's a lot easier to put yourself out there and have new dating experiences when you feel confident in yourself.

Improving Your Relationships

You may find that your relationships suffer when you don't feel confident in yourself. When you are filled with insecurities and anxieties about yourself, you are more likely to project this onto the people you date, which causes these relationships to suffer. This makes it important to work on your relationship with yourself so that it can improve the romantic relationships you may have. These are some ways being confident within yourself can help your romantic relationship:

- **You are more confident in the relationship.** When you lack confidence in yourself, you will find yourself riddled with insecurities. This will cause you to create issues in your relationship because you feel insecure about yourself. When you're insecure within yourself, you will also have trust issues. You believe that the person you're with may cheat on you or end up hurting you in some way because you think you're not good enough for them. Having confidence will help you to be a better partner because you won't continuously overthink and question your relationship.

- **You are a happier partner.** Being a confident person can help you to be a happier partner that people actually want to be around. You will find yourself feeling a lot more fulfilled in life, which makes you a better partner. When you're happy, you find it easier to be yourself and fully embrace both your strengths and weaknesses. This makes you a great partner, as you are able to take care of yourself and love yourself in a healthy manner. In return, this helps you to spread love and happiness to the people you date.

- **You have your own identity.** Sometimes being in a relationship, especially for a long time, can cause you to lose a sense of yourself. You get so comfortable in your relationship that you can't live without the other person. Your identity becomes combined with your partner as you are codependent with them. When you enter a relationship with confidence, you're able to realize you're both individuals with your own identities. Having your own identity helps you to be a better partner because you don't put too much pressure on your relationship. You're also able to cope being by yourself, which is crucial if you want to be in a healthy relationship.

You Choose the Right Relationships

Having confidence in yourself doesn't only help you to improve the relationships you already have, but it also helps you to seek out the right type of relationships in your life. When you're confident in yourself, you're able to find love for who you are. This helps you to choose the right relationships in your life because you don't attract the toxic individuals who end up hurting you.

When you have low self-esteem, it can cause you to be attracted to the wrong type of people. You think that you deserve someone toxic who doesn't actually care about you. This causes you to accept when you are treated badly because you think that it's acceptable treatment for you.

Being confident in yourself helps you to raise your standards as you realize you deserve so much more from a partner. You know your worth because your confidence allows you to see all of your positive characteristics. This means that you seek individuals who will make you happy and bring value to your life.

Improving Your Sex Life

One of the reasons why confidence is so important when you're dating is because it can have a major impact on your sex life. If you're just looking to improve your sex life, then confidence is a major factor. Before you go out into the world trying to improve your sex life, you need to be able to find confidence within yourself first. If you feel like something is missing in your sex life, then having confidence can help you to alleviate this issue. These are a few ways confidence can improve your sex life:

- **You feel more comfortable.** A reason why you may struggle in the bedroom is because you feel uncomfortable. You don't want to put yourself out there in that way because it makes you feel weird. You may end up having sex just because you know the person you're with wants to, rather than doing it because you, yourself, want to. When you're confident in yourself, you're more likely to make a confident decision with sex. You either want to explore having sexual relations with someone, or you are confident in saying no to someone.

- **You feel interested in exploring new things.** Another way confidence can improve your sex life is by making you open to exploring new things. You may have some sexual desires that you want to participate in but you're always too nervous to implement them. You don't know how your partner will react and whether you'll be able to execute it properly. This is why it's important to build your confidence, as you will feel more capable of being adventurous with your sex life.

- **You feel more confident vocalizing yourself.** When it comes to conversations about sex, many of us feel nervous to vocalize what we like and don't like, as well as whether or not we're comfortable. Being confident in yourself helps you to gain the courage to vocalize what you're feeling sexually. If you want to suggest something you want to do with your partner, you'll let them know, and if you want to vocalize something you're not comfortable with, you have the confidence to set boundaries with assertiveness.

Your sex life makes up a big part of your love life, so it's important to feel confident within it. You don't have to settle for uncomfortable and boring sexual experiences, because you can use your confidence to experience maximum pleasure. We will discuss sex and intimacy in a lot more detail further on in the book if you need tips to help you spice up your love life.

Beginners' Nerves

It's very common for newbie daters to find themselves overwhelmed with anxiety, fear, and insecurities. You haven't put yourself out there in a while, so you have a fear of getting rejected or hurt. You may think that you aren't good enough to get the love that you so deeply desire. Everyone has beginners' nerves, but it's important for you to realize that these uncomfortable feelings will pass with time.

Stay Present in the Moment

For many people who experience anxiety and beginner's nerves when dating, they find themselves consumed by their minds. This means that they're constantly overthinking and their mind is always traveling to the negatives. When you get so consumed by your thoughts and what could happen, it distracts you from the present moment.

This is why it's so important for you to work on staying present in the moment. Being present in the moment of your date can also make your dating experiences more enjoyable, as you are focused on what happens as it happens. This helps you to avoid psyching yourself up to the point that your date becomes unenjoyable. These are some ways you can learn how to stay present in the moment:

- **Tap into your physical senses.** A great way for you to stay focused on the current moment you're experiencing is by taking special note of your physical senses. When you take a second to breathe and notice what's stimulating your senses, it can help you to become a lot more present in the moment. You can take a note of what exactly you're looking at when you look at them. Maybe they have a really mesmerizing smile. Or, you could be taking note of their scent, which is unique and attractive. Focusing on your senses can bring you back to Earth, as it prevents you from being too distracted mentally.

- **Put your phone on airplane mode.** If you find yourself being anxious or scared on your date, you may find that you end up going on your phone to distract yourself. It can be so easy to just go on your phone when you feel as though you're on a really awkward date. Although going on your phone may provide you with comfort, it can be detrimental for your date. This is why it's better for you to put your phone on airplane mode so you don't feel tempted and distracted.

- **Listen and ask questions.** To avoid getting too side tracked on the date, the best thing for you to do is to focus on what your date is saying. If you feel like you're getting distracted on your date and you find yourself feeling too anxious, then taking the time to listen attentively will bring back your attention. You can even ask questions that will help you to feel more engaged and interested in the conversation. Listening is the best way to distract yourself from your own anxious thoughts.

Once you master being present in the moment, you'll be able to become a dating master. When you're on a date with someone, it's valuable to know how to focus on them so that you can both have the most engaging and enjoyable experience together. After going on a few dates where you stay focused, you'll realize that dating isn't as scary as you may think it is.

Practice Makes Perfect

Dating is like everything else in life: the more you do it, the less anxious you may feel about it. However, you need to avoid becoming a serial dater, as this can become unhealthy for you. It becomes mentally draining and toxic when you find yourself going on numerous dates, one after the other. You need to pace yourself by taking breaks and going on dates with people you really want to see.

With that being said, going on a date once a week or once every other week won't hurt. You may find that you benefit a lot from going on dates every now and then, as you feel more comfortable with dating. This will help you to approach each date with a sense of calmness that helps you to be successful.

How to Build Dating Confidence

You may feel scared and fearful of entering the dating world because you've lost confidence in yourself and your ability to date successfully. Going on dates, meeting new people, and putting yourself out there can be very nerve wracking, but it can feel a lot more manageable when you build confidence within yourself. These are some tips and tricks that can help you to build the confidence to do dating right.

Create a Pre-Date Routine

Psyching yourself up for a date can be the most nerve wracking part of going on a date, especially when it's a first date with someone you're not that familiar with. This is why it's valuable to create a pre-date routine that mentally prepares you for your date ahead. This routine can get you into a positive mindset, as you calm down and get excited for the new experience ahead of you.

Your pre-date routine can be anything that makes you happy and calm. Here is an example of a pre-date routine that you can use (or it can inspire you to create your own routine):

1. **Bath or shower.** Your pre-date routine should start a few hours before your date so that you can feel properly prepared. You can start off this routine by taking a nice long hot shower or bath. A bath may be more preferable, as you can lie down and relax. You can add bath salts and even have a bubble bath to create a soothing atmosphere for yourself. You can also play some relaxing music as you bathe, which can influence you to calm down.

2. **Talk to a friend.** A great way to calm your nerves before a date is by talking to a good friend. You may also find that you have so much time before a date that you don't know what to do. You can't do anything productive because you feel too anxious, so having a small chat over the phone with a friend is a great time waster. You can even ask for a pep talk from your friend that helps you to feel more confident in yourself.

3. **Watch something enjoyable.** If you're not the type who wants to talk to a friend before a date because you prefer to keep your love life to yourself, then try to do another activity you enjoy. Maybe you can watch a funny, distracting show to pass time, or you can read a good book. This is a great activity to do if you have some extra time you want to waste before your date.

4. **Get ready.** Once you're getting closer to date time, it's time to start getting ready. This can be the most fun part of the routine, as you have the opportunity to make yourself feel good and confident. When you're getting ready, you want to make yourself look as attractive as possible, which means you put on your best outfit, style your hair, put makeup on, and wear cologne or perfume. Once you are looking your best, it will make you feel so much more confident to go on a date. As you get ready, you should also take the opportunity to repeat positive affirmations to yourself in the mirror. For example, you can tell yourself, "I look good and I will have an amazing date." This will give you an extra confidence boost.

5. **Do breathing exercises.** When you're ready to leave the house and go on a date, you may find that your feelings of anxiety and nervousness begin to intensify. If you find yourself still feeling nervous, then you can practice some breathing exercises that will calm down your nerves before you leave for your date. Start by breathing into the count of three and then proceed by breathing out to the

count of three. You can repeat this process, and while you breathe, think positive thoughts about your date. After this, you will feel calmer and ready to take on your date.

Consider How Great You Are as a Date

You may feel nervous and less confident to date because you feel as though you aren't worthy of dating. No matter who you are, it's important to realize that there's someone out there for you. Whether you believe it or not, you have some amazing strengths and qualities that make you a great individual to date. This is why you should take time to consider what would make you a great partner. The following are a few ways you can consider for determining what makes you a good partner:

- **Make a list of your strengths.** A great way to give yourself a confidence boost is by writing down a list of all the strengths you're proud of having. This is when you do some self-aware thinking, as you think of all of your positive qualities that make you special and great. Consider your more favorable characteristics which make you a positive person to be around. When you make this list, don't be shy and modest, as you need to be honest with yourself.

- **Talk to friends and family.** Sometimes it's challenging to see the strengths and positive qualities within ourselves. We're so used to being pessimistic and negative that we don't realize all the great aspects of ourselves that would make us a great date. Asking your friends and family members about the positive aspects of yourself can surprise you, as you may find out a lot you were never aware of.

- **Ask the person you're dating.** You may think it's a bit tacky to ask the person you're dating what they think of you, but there are ways you can do this tastefully. Firstly, you must avoid blatantly asking for someone's opinion of you, instead, you can be more discreet and casual about it. For example, you can start off by complimenting the person you're talking to by letting them know the strengths you admire in them. Then, once they receive these compliments, you can ask in return how they feel. You may be surprised to find the positive things your date says about you and it can provide you with a great positive boost.

You need to have more confidence in your ability to conquer the dating world because at the end of the day, it's all in your control. You may not be able to see it in yourself, but you are an amazing dating candidate, as you have unique positive qualities that make you desirable.

Prepare Questions

Another reason why you may have a lack of confidence when you're dating is because you're scared of awkward silences, you don't know how to start conversations, and you fear you won't be prepared for what's to come. Unfortunately, you can't fully prepare for a date because you can't predict what other people will say to you. The best way you can prepare yourself for a date is by preparing a set of questions you can ask when a conversation gets dry and awkward.

When you find yourself in an awkward stage of a conversation and you don't know how to communicate further, you can create a list of questions that can be used as an icebreaker.

These are examples of interesting questions you can ask to feel more prepared for a date:

- *Do you have an interesting secret about yourself?* Often on dates, people get caught in the trap of asking bland and uninteresting questions. When you ask these boring questions, such as, "Can you tell me about yourself?", you not only get uninteresting responses but you may end up boring your date. This is why it's important to ask more intriguing and interesting questions such as this one. Asking about a secret someone might have can instigate exciting conversation.

- *Who are the important people in your life?* When you're on a date with someone, you want to give them the impression that you want to learn more about them and their life. To accomplish this, you need to ask questions that help you learn what's important to them. By asking who the important people in their life are, you learn about them on a deeper level. You will also find that they get more passionate as they speak to you.

- *What are some random facts about yourself?* Sometimes the easiest way to learn more about others is by straight up asking them facts about themselves. Instead of asking someone what their hobbies are, what they can tell you about themselves, or what their passions are, you can ask a more broad question like this. Asking for random facts provides them with the freedom to share and talk about anything they're comfortable with.

- *What's the worst date you've ever been on?* A question that can help to lighten the mood is this one. If you feel like your date is too serious and you're engaging in formal conversation, you may want to bring up a fun topic that can lead to some laughter. Asking your date about their worst dating experience can inspire storytelling from both of you. They may share a funny story you could relate to or laugh at. This also provides you with an opportunity to share a funny story of your own.

Don't Put So Much Pressure on Yourself

You may feel less confident dating because you put so much pressure on yourself. You continuously worry about whether the other person will like you or not, which makes you unnecessarily stressed for a date. You begin to overthink whether you look good enough, if you're funny enough, or whether you're good company. This mindset can make you feel insecure as you approach a date.

It's all about having the right mindset that doesn't make you feel overwhelmed and negative when you're going on a date. If you go into a date thinking that you need to be perfect, you're bound to feel anxious and overwhelmed. This is why it's important for you to take each date as it comes with a positive healthy attitude. This is how you can feel more confident when you approach a date:

- **Consider if you like the person.** You get so preoccupied thinking whether the person you're dating likes you that you fail to consider whether you even like them in return. Although it's important to be accommodating to the people we date to ensure that they're comfortable, you should still think of your own needs and desires. Ask yourself whether you actually like the person you're dating, as they may not even tick the boxes you want. If you're not that interested in your date, take it as an opportunity to practice your dating skills stress free, because you have less pressure to feel like you need to be perfect.

- **Have low expectations.** The worst thing you can do when you're going on a date is have high expectations that everything will be perfect. If you work yourself up with high expectations by thinking that your date is going to be amazing and you're meeting the love of your life, you face the risk of being massively disappointed. This can also make you more anxious, as you feel like you need to create the perfect date. When you have low expectations, you feel less pressure to be the perfect date. You'll also find that your date goes a lot better than you expected, which will make you feel happy and comfortable.

- **Consider the worst case scenario.** If having low expectations doesn't help you, you should try to think of the worst case scenario that can happen on this date. Sometimes thinking about the worst things that can happen shows you that there's actually nothing to worry about. Having a bad date won't kill you. The worst thing that can happen is that you feel awkward and uncomfortable for a moment, which will be an amusing story later in your life.

- **Remember there will be more dates.** Even if your date does happen to become the worst case scenario, you need to remember that there will be plenty more dates in your life. When you're going on a date you may feel like this is it, which puts more pressure on yourself. You need to realize that you will have many more opportunities to date, so if this isn't a good date, it really isn't the end of the world. You're bound to experience a marvelous date one day with someone meant for you, so don't put pressure on yourself to make every date perfect.

Dating is meant to be fun and enjoyable, so you shouldn't ruin this experience for yourself by applying too much pressure on yourself. Approach each dating experience with courage and confidence because that's when you'll end up having the best experience. When you put less pressure on yourself, you'll find it easier to tackle each date with confidence.

Chapter 4:

Love Hypnosis and Telepathy

Hypnotherapy is when your conscious mind is quieted, while your subconscious mind comes to focus. When someone practices hypnotherapy on you, they're able to tap into a deeper part of your brain, without you being actively aware of it. You may find that you have mental blocks that prevent you from pursuing dating.

Another great way to approach your fear and anxiety toward dating is by tapping into telepathy. Being able to use telepathy with a partner can help connect the both of you on a deeper level. You're able to understand each other and communicate without having to say a word.

Using Hypnotherapy for Your Love Life

This may seem like a strange and unconventional way to attract the love and partner you desire in your life, but it is a lot more effective than you may realize. Using hypnotherapy can help you to overcome deeper issues that you may struggle to address consciously.

We all have some deep-rooted habits that can negatively impact our dating lives. If you try to approach these issues on your own and fail to see any progress, then it may be valuable for you to pursue hypnotherapy in order to address these issues.

These are some personal issues you may have that can be successfully conquered by hypnosis:

- **Anxiety and stress.** One of the things that can be detrimental to your dating game is being too anxious and stressed. When you have the first date nerves, it can cause you to fumble and act strangely on your date. Your date won't be able to see your true positive nature because you're too anxious and nervous. Doing new things and getting out of your comfort zone may threaten you, but practicing hypnosis can help you to feel less stressed out and overwhelmed.

- **Phobias.** Do you have any phobias that make you too fearful to put yourself out there in the dating world? You may have some trust issues and phobias of commitment or getting hurt that prevent you from pursuing dating successfully. If dating is a fear of yours because you're scared of being rejected, practicing love hypnosis will help you to have a more positive approach toward dating. You will begin to trust more, especially if you've been hurt badly in the past.

- **Behavioral control issues.** If you have behavioral control issues that prevent you from living a normal life and pursuing your love life, then hypnosis can help you to manage these issues. You may have unhealthy addictions that control your life such as alcohol or drug abuse. When you use hypnosis, you can get rid of these unhealthy habits that set you back from pursuing dating.

Once you're able to conquer these personal issues, you will be able to pursue dating with more confidence. Sometimes we are our own enemies, as we are scared about putting ourselves out there. When you work on yourself holistically and eliminate those mental blocks, you will be able to date successfully.

How It Works

If you want to use hypnotherapy to conquer your fears of dating, you need to visit a professional hypnotherapist. This is an activity that is possible to do on your own, and if you ask a friend or family member, it may not be effective at all. A trained professional knows how to practice hypnosis effectively and safely. Here is what you'll go through if you visit a hypnotherapist:

1. **Induction.** This process starts off with you being induced into a calm and meditative state by your hypnotherapist. By using specific techniques like deep breathing, muscle relaxation, or focusing on a visual image, your hypnotherapist can focus your attention.

2. **Deepener.** Once you are attentive and falling into a focused state, your therapist will want you to be relaxed on a deeper level. You need to be in a deep focused state so that your subconscious mind can be more open and receptive. They want your conscious mind to be inactive during this process so that they can instruct your subconscious mind.

3. **Suggestions.** After you reach a completely relaxed state where you're more open to instructions, your therapist will introduce you to instructions. This is where the real hypnotherapy comes into play, as your therapist provides your subconscious mind with verbal instructions. These instructions will work on resolving your problem,

discovering what triggers it, and exploring it. Over time, you will notice that your issue begins to fade away.

4. **Emergence.** Once the hypnotherapy is complete, your therapist will slowly work on emerging you out of your hypnotic state. This is where your therapist reverses their deepener strategies that put you in a deep trance, so you can be fully conscious again. They do this slowly and gradually with specific techniques such as climbing up the stairs visually or counting.

Things You Should Know

Before you go out and embark on this form of hypnosis, it's important for you to know a few things before you practice it. It's important to have a realistic idea of what love hypnosis is before you get involved in it. You don't want to have unrealistic expectations, and you also don't want to misuse it in your life. These are a few facts you need to know before getting started with hypnotherapy:

- **It's not magic.** Although hypnotherapy is effective and relatively quick and easy, it isn't magic. You may be used to what you've seen on live stage shows or on television, but love hypnosis isn't as drastic. It may take up to 21 days for your love hypnosis to actually create habits within you. You need to be patient when you practice hypnotherapy because you can't expect results to occur overnight.

- **Hypnotherapists aren't doctors.** You may be using hypnotherapy to combat relationship trauma or issues you've faced, but it's important to know that they aren't licensed doctors. They won't help you to get rid of your problems, but rather, they'll help you to remove any mental blockages that are preventing you from pursuing the love you desire.

- **You aren't asleep during hypnosis.** If you've seen hypnosis happen, you may be under the impression that you're asleep when you're practicing hypnotherapy. Although your eyes may be closed and you're not behaving consciously, you're not sleeping. Your mind is in an extreme state of calm and you're able to hear everything you're being told.

Hypnotherapy may be exactly what you need to get out of your mental trap that prevents you from being the best version of yourself. It's important to try and conquer your phobias and fears on your own, but if that doesn't work, trying love hypnosis will get you in the right frame of mind to fall in love.

How to Practice Telepathy

You've conquered your fear of dating and you're ready to put yourself out there. You find an amazing date who you see as a potential partner, so you want to find a way to connect with them on a deeper level. One way you can do this is by tapping into your psychic abilities. You and your future partner have the potential to connect on a psychic level by practicing telepathy through following these steps:

1. **Enter a meditative state.** To practice telepathy so that you can connect and communicate with your partner, you need to get into a meditative state first. Whatever you need to do to focus and reach a calm state—do it!

You can meditate, practice yoga, or practice deep breathing.

2. **Send a small message.** Once you get into this meditative state, you'll be able to send a small message to your partner. Think of a short message or phrase to deliver to your partner. Focus on these words and imagine them entering your partner's mind. Go through this process again and again until you know your partner has received it.

3. **Send a mental image.** After you've successfully managed to focus and send a message to your partner, you should send a mental image. Think of something beautiful that represents your love with them. Focus on this image intensely and imagine it entering your partner's mind.

4. **Be patient.** When you're starting off with telepathy, you mustn't rush the process. You may get frustrated because you don't see results, but with time and practice, you will be able to successfully practice telepathy. It's all about being focused and in tune with your psychic abilities.

It may sound unrealistic to you, but you do have psychic abilities. Our minds are a lot more powerful than we give them credit for. If you work on your telepathy skills every day, you will be surprised how powerful your relationship can become through the work of your mind!

Chapter 5:

Improve Your Sex Life

You may be wanting to improve your love life because you're tired of having a boring and dry sex life. There are always ways to spice up your sex life, whether you're single or currently in a relationship with someone. Many people view sex as something forbidden to explore freely, but if you have an open mind, you can have sex a lot more enjoyable for both you and your partner.

Working on Intimacy

When it comes to transforming your sex life, we're not only going to talk about sex, but we need to talk about intimacy too. It can be easy to forget that intimacy plays a major role in having a successful sex life. If you want to improve your sex with someone, you need to work toward building your intimate relationship with them.

How Intimate Are You?

Intimacy can be seen as a spectrum because some of us are more intimate than others. There are many different types of intimacy expressions and different degrees in which people express it. If you want to work on having more solid and successful relationships with people, you need to understand your type and level of intimacy. A great way for you to discover how intimate you are is by considering the four types of intimacy. These are:

1. **Physical intimacy.** When we talk about physical intimacy, the first thing you may think of is sex, but intimacy is about a lot more than just sex. Physical intimacy is about physical touch, cuddling, kissing, holding hands, and many other things. You need to consider how often you express affection physically, because this will show how intimate you are on a physical and sexual level.

2. **Emotional intimacy.** You may find that you're less into physical intimacy because you're not the type to be very affectionate. If this is the case for you, then you may be more interested in emotional intimacy in a relationship. You value that emotional connection with someone because it makes you feel comfortable and safe. This means that you bond over private thoughts and feelings, sharing information about your traumatic life experiences, and expressing how you feel to each other.

3. **Intellectual intimacy.** Another form of connection that you may value and prioritize is an intellectual bond. You may want to be in a relationship with someone you share opinions and beliefs with. You may value the type of relationship where you can engage in intellectual conversations frequently. Having intellectual compatibility with someone can make your relationship a lot stronger.

4. **Experimental intimacy.** The last type of intimacy you can consider is experimental intimacy. This type of intimacy is achieved by simply experiencing things with your partner. A great relationship is one where you're able to do lots of enjoyable things together. When you experience things together, it also helps you to build a

stronger bond, as you enjoy your time spent with each other.

At the end of the day, if you want to improve your intimacy, you want to work toward being intimate in all aspects. This can be challenging to do because you may find that one level of intimacy makes you more comfortable and happy. So, it's important for you to embrace the type of intimacy that feels like love to you. You may be struggling to determine how intimate you truly are, so these are some signs that you are a more intimate individual:

- **You're vulnerable in a relationship.** A sign that you're an intimate person is if you're able to be vulnerable when you find yourself in a relationship. You're able to showcase your weaknesses and emotions because you feel comfortable with the people you date. Emotional intimacy is something easy for you to achieve because you are quite open and vulnerable.

- **You're interdependent in a relationship.** Being interdependent means that you have a healthy relationship with the people you date. This interdependent relationship is specifically formed through teamwork within your relationship, as you work together and communicate as a unit. This helps you to have a stronger connection with your partner.

- **You're honest and trusting.** Having raw honesty in a relationship shows that you are able to be unapologetically intimate with someone. When you're able to open up honestly and show the raw side of yourself, it demonstrates that you're able to grow your emotional connections. You're also able to get closer to your partner, as you break down your emotional walls that are guarding you from being in love.

59

If you can relate to any of these signs, then this could be an indicator that you are a more intimate person, which may be shown in your affection or vulnerability in your relationships. Being more intimate has the power to help you in many ways, so don't be afraid to embrace this vulnerability. You may not think that embracing all these different types of intimacy will improve your sex life, but you'd be surprised to discover what they can do for the sexual part of your relationships.

How to Be More Intimate

If you're trying to become more intimate in a relationship, then you should be open to getting out of your comfort zone. To embrace intimacy, you may need to do things that go against your usual character, but it will all be worth it in the end. Some of us are more intimate than others and this could be due to a number of reasons. For example, you may be a more intimate person if you grew up with a family that's affectionate and intimate in a healthy manner.

Whether intimacy is something you're familiar with or not, we're all capable of embracing this softer side of ourselves. Once you begin being more intimate in a relationship, you will see how beneficial it can be for your love life. These are some tips that will help you to be a more intimate person regardless of who you are:

- **Go on romantic dates.** When you're in a relationship and you want to keep the passion and love alive between the two of you, you need to make time for romantic dates. When you're with someone for long, it can be easy to get into the routine of staying home, eating fast food, and watching Netflix, but you need to keep the intimacy and romance alive by going on romantic dates that spark passion.

- **Don't be shy to be flirtatious.** If you want to improve your intimacy, you need to work on being confident to make the first move sometimes. If you're constantly waiting for someone to make the first intimate move with you, you will struggle to get this relationship to the next level. When you are flirty and touchy with your partner or date, it sets a tone of intimacy that the other person can follow.

- **Embark on adventures together.** Along with going on romantic dates, you need to create new experiences with your partner because this can help you to bond on a deeper level. Having new experiences with your partner can help you to keep your spark alive, as well as bringing an element of excitement into your dating life which can help you to build intimacy.

- **Don't be scared of being vulnerable.** As established before, being vulnerable is an important part of building intimacy because it's impossible to build intimacy when you have walls built up around you. You may struggle to be vulnerable as you see it as a sign of weakness, but this couldn't be further from the truth. If you want to become more vulnerable, you need to be open to sharing your negative circumstances, characteristics, and feelings. Be open to showing the imperfect side of yourself.

Although it's important to be vulnerable and intimate in your dating life, you also need to have boundaries that prevent you from getting hurt. Unfortunately, there are toxic individuals out there with the wrong intentions who don't deserve your intimacy and vulnerability. They will take advantage of it and end up hurting you in the long run. If you want to learn how to discover who to be vulnerable with, you can use the WAIT method to guide you. This stands for the following:

- **Want** - When you're thinking of sharing vulnerable information with someone you're dating, you should start off by considering whether this is information you indeed want to share with them. You don't have to share information that you're uncomfortable with revealing just because you want to appeal to the vulnerable. Only show vulnerabilities you want to share with a person you feel comfortable with.

- **Appropriate** - Sharing vulnerable and personal information is not appropriate for just any old time, so you need to consider whether it's truly a good time to open up about something close to you. You can do this by considering the tone and context of the conversation you're currently having. You don't want to bring up a serious topic at an inappropriate time that makes the conversation awkward or toxic. They may react negatively, which can make you feel insecure about yourself and your vulnerabilities.

- **Inoculate** - When you do feel as though you're ready to share personal information with someone, you shouldn't just throw it all at them at once. You need to introduce them to your vulnerabilities slowly, so they can get an idea of what you deal with. You can then start progressively opening up so that it's not too overwhelming for both you and the person you're opening up to.

- **Trust** - If you want to share something vulnerable, you need to make sure you trust the person you're dating. It's not wise to share your deepest darkest secrets with every individual you date because this can turn out negatively. Instead, you should share this intimate side of yourself with a partner or date you trust because then it'll strengthen your relationship with them, rather than destroy it.

The Importance of a Healthy Sex Life

Whether we like to believe it or not, having a healthy sex life has a massive impact on your love life. You want to be able to build a strong connection with the people you date, and this connection can only be built with intimacy. We all know that a big part of intimacy is your sex life, so this is why it's valuable for you to know how you can elevate it. Sex isn't everything, but it can be beneficial for your love life in the following ways:

- **It strengthens your bond.** One of the main reasons why a healthy sex life is important for your relationship is because it strengthens your bond with your partner. When you have sex with someone, you will connect on a deeper level. Your bond grows as you feel more connected to that person. You may find that you become stronger than ever, especially if you're connected to this person emotionally and mentally first.

- **It reduces conflict.** If you find yourself constantly in conflict with your partner, you may find that improving your sex life alleviates this issue. Sometimes, sexual tension between you and another person can cause you two to butt heads constantly. Being sexually active helps you to relieve this tension, as well as be a lot softer and more affectionate with the other person. Ultimately, this will reduce conflict between you and the person you're dating.

- **It improves your health.** Having a healthy amount of sex doesn't only help your relationship; it also helps your overall health and happiness as an individual. It's been proven that having sex regularly can improve your heart health, help you burn calories, boost your immune system, and reduce pain you experience. This can make you an overall healthier and happier person.

- **It reduces stress.** Having regular sex also helps you to reduce your stress, which can help you to improve your overall happiness. If you manage to reduce the stress you experience on a daily basis, you will notice that it improves your relationship. Being overly stressed can take a toll on your relationship as you end up taking it out on your partner and the people you date.

It's so important not to prioritize sex in your relationship or your dating life, because it's not what keeps a relationship together. Although it's not the most important aspect of a relationship or date, it does make up an important part of it. Why not make the most of your sex life by making your relationship better, as well as improving your own quality of life?

How to Improve Your Sex Life

You're tired of your same boring sex life and it feels like there's no passion or fire between you and your partner. We all experience dry spells in our sex life, whether we're in a relationship or we're singles. There are various ways you can improve your sex life, as you don't have to settle for inadequacy.

Improving Your Sex Life While Single

Before we discuss how you can improve your sex life in your relationship, you may want to learn about how you can transform your sex life as a single person who is dating. It can be challenging to have a sex life when you're just dating, because you need to find individuals who are on the same page as you. These are some tips that will help you to successfully transform your sex life as a single person:

- **Ensure everything is consensual.** Before considering any tips to improve your sexual dating life, you need to ensure you're approaching this lifestyle in a healthy manner. You should only be having consensual sex with the people you date. This means that you shouldn't force someone to do anything they don't want to do. You shouldn't try to persuade them to fulfill your sexual desires if they seem uncomfortable, tell you no, or seem hesitant. Sex should be enjoyable and consensual for both parties.

- **Find people with the same intentions.** To find people with the same intentions as you, you need to make your intentions clear when you date. Let them know that having sex while you date is something that you're interested in. If this is something they're not looking for, then you can part ways; but if they are comfortable with it, they can be an optimal partner to date. When you're dating someone who is also interested in pursuing a sexual relationship, you need to ensure that you're on the same page.

- **Put yourself out there.** If you want to look for someone with the same intentions and desires as you, you need to put yourself out there. Unfortunately, the perfect dates aren't just going to fall in your lap, so you need to put in the work. You need to be able to put yourself out there to find the right people to date. You can consider going on Tinder or even approaching strangers and asking them out. In the next chapter, we will explore how you can put yourself out there and find the right people to date.

- **Don't use people for sex.** The worst thing you can do if you're pursuing casual dating is to use the people you date for sex. If you're dating someone, you can't pretend to have deeper feelings just to end up just using them for sex and dumping them afterward. This is why it's important to be clear about your intentions. If someone is looking for a deeper relationship and you're attracted to them, don't deceive them just to get what you want.

Remember when you're single and dating, you shouldn't make sex your only and biggest priority. There's so much you can get out of dating, so don't just use your dates for their bodies. You need to respect the people you date and explore your sex life with class. The rest of this section will now uncover how you can improve your sex life within a relationship.

Have a Conversation With Your Partner

When you're trying to improve your sex life with your partner, it's important to start off this journey by having an open conversation with them. Sex is a two-way activity, so you need to be on the same page with everything you do. If you feel like you've been lacking passion lately and you want to improve your intimacy and elevate your sexual experiences, then have an open and honest conversation with them. These tips will help you to engage in this conversation in the best way possible:

- **Reassure your partner.** When you want to let your partner know that you want to improve your sex life with them, you need to word it very carefully. You don't want to come off insensitive, as this may result in offending them. Assure them that you love sex with them, but you have some ideas to make it even better. Never make them feel inadequate sexually, as this will create a massive obstacle in your relationship.

- **Voice your suggestions.** Once you've reassured your partner that you're happy with them, you can pursue this conversation. Voice the sexual desires and needs that you feel can be worked on in your relationship and ask how your partner feels about them. Remember that for some people certain sexual activities make them uncomfortable. If you suggest something and your partner is uncomfortable, respect their wishes and don't make a big deal out of it. Your suggestions should merely be potential add-ons to your sex life; not something that will make or break your relationship.

- **Ensure that it's a safe space to speak.** You also want it to be a safe space for your partner to speak, as you may find that they have suggestions they've been wanting to bring to the table. Once you're done sharing your suggestions, ask your partner what they want from your sex life together so that they can be more satisfied. This will make them feel like it's something you can work on together, instead of them feeling targeted. Your partner may provide you with criticism and you should be prepared to listen to it with an open mind. You need to create a safe space where you can both be open about your sexual needs and desires so that you can have a mature conversation about them.

We can often make conversations about sex a lot more awkward and forbidden than they need to be. Having conversations about your sex life shouldn't intimidate you, rather, they should empower you and your relationship. These conversations can do so much for you and can become a regular occasion for you. After you try new things, you can have more conversations to see how both of you feel. Keeping up your communication will ultimately result in a happy and successful sex life.

Improve Your Fitness

If you want to elevate and transform your sex life, you should work on improving your overall fitness. Being sexual is a physical activity within itself, as it can take a lot of stamina, muscle, and energy, especially if you want to try advanced moves. If you want to stray away from the boring and typical positions and activities, then you need to ensure your fitness is on par.

You can do small things to improve your fitness like practicing cardio by going for walks and jogs frequently. Depending on what you want to explore sexually, you can work out different parts of your body. Being fit can also help you to get your body where you want it to be aesthetically. This can make you feel more confident when you engage in sexual activities.

Be Adventurous

One of the best ways to spice up your sex life is by being adventurous. You need to explore new sexual activities because you may find yourself stuck in a sexual routine with your partner. Although it may get the job done, after a while your partner may find this tedious and monotonous. You need to spice up the relationship with new activities and adventurous sex. Here are a few ways you can be adventurous with your partner in your sex life:

- **Educate yourself.** You may find that you don't know a lot about sex and how to be adventurous, and if so, you can find ways to educate yourself. There's lots of knowledge out there about how to enhance your sexual life. You can get advice from a sex coach who knows what they're talking about. You can also hire a professional or find affordable resources on the internet.

- **Use foreplay.** A great way to spice up your sex life is by making use of foreplay. This is where you can really explore different fantasies with your partner. Foreplay is when you spend time before having sex building up a storyline or scene. This can create sexual tension and build up excitement, which makes the actual sexual activity more thrilling. You can explore fantasies with your partner that you've always desired.

- **Play with your senses.** We often take our senses for granted, but they can actually help you to enhance your sexual experiences. By taking away your senses or enhancing them, you may find that you experience an extremely thrilling experience. For example, you can blindfold yourself or your partner as you have sex, as this will add more tension to the experience. You could also add the sense of taste to your sexual experience, by using chocolate on each other.

When it comes to sex, there are so many different ways for you to be adventurous. You don't even have to prepare yourself for it because you can just go with the flow. You may find that winging it with your partner leads to the best results because you end up embracing the sexiest versions of yourselves.

Don't Do Anything You Wouldn't Be Comfortable With

Above all, it's important for you to explore what makes you comfortable in your sex life. You should never feel pressured to engage in something you're uncomfortable with, even if everyone else you know has done it already. Unfortunately, there are people who can apply pressure to you, manipulate, and guilt-trip you into doing things you aren't comfortable with.

If you're being asked to do something sexually and you feel hesitant, consider to yourself whether you're comfortable with it or not. If you aren't comfortable, then you shouldn't be afraid to say "no." When you say "no" to them, you must be assertive and sure about how you feel. The person you're dating may feel compelled to convince you or persuade you about how you feel, but you should be firm in your feelings.

At the end of the day, you're in control of your sex life. If you aren't ready to have casual sex, you don't have to. If you're uncomfortable with a request from your partner, you can say "no," and if you are creeped out by someone you're dating, you can leave them. It's all in your control, so don't feel guilty or scared about avoiding sexual activities that make you feel discomfort.

Chapter 6:

How to Find the Right Partner

If you're on the search to find your soulmate or dream partner, you may be struggling to find someone who aligns with everything you desire from a partner. Learning how to find the right partner can be challenging, especially in the current dating pool that is filled with toxic people who are just looking for meaningless hookups. You need to know how to find the right partners so that you prevent yourself from falling into a harmful trap that leaves you heartbroken.

On the other hand, you may be looking for something more casual and lighthearted, so it's important to know the right person to pick for this type of relationship as well. You don't want to end up hurting someone and using them when they are looking for something serious. You'd be surprised to know how many people are looking for different things in the dating world. All you need to do is know where to look and learn how to find the right one.

Know What You're Looking For

The easiest way for you to find the right partner is by having a specific idea of what you're looking for in a partner. Having an idea of what you're looking for can help you decide where you must look and how you should go about dating. When you know what you want from a partner, you will ensure that you both are pursuing the same thing that makes you happy.

Have High Standards

It's crucial to have high standards when you're dating because you want to find someone who treats you well. If you have a lower self-esteem and you're critical of yourself, it can cause you to lower your standards. This means that you hate people who don't have your best interest at heart.

When you start thinking about what you want from a partner, you must be honest with yourself, instead of saying you just want anyone. You are worthy of high standards, especially when you bring a lot of positives to a relationship. You deserve a healthy relationship that makes you feel happy and fulfilled, so don't feel silly for aiming high when you're looking for a partner.

Reconsider Your Dream Partner

Earlier on in this book, you decided who your dream partner may be. Now's the time for you to rethink this. If you're actively searching for a partner who will make you happy, then you should remember all the qualities and interests of your dream partner that you've thought of.

When you start dating, you should remember the idea of this dream partner, as it can help you to determine whether you've met someone who fits your desires or not. You're able to remind yourself of what you've been looking for in a partner, so you don't settle for less.

Consider Common Interests and Values

One thing that could be valuable to you is sharing common interests with your partner. Having common interests with a partner is important as it can help you to bond over something. You will find that it helps you to have a more solid relationship with someone because you're able to relate with each other on a deeper level. These are some questions you can ask yourself to consider what interests are important for you in your future relationship:

- *What are some of my most important interests?* Start off by determining what some of your main interests are that mean the most to you. Knowing what interests you value the most will help you to determine what's most important to you. You may expect your partner to relate with you on your more valuable interests.

- *Do I want a partner with similar hobbies?* You can then ask yourself if you want to pursue a relationship with someone who has the same hobbies as you. You may want to be with someone who is interested in similar hobbies because then you can bond over them and participate in these activities together. On the other hand, you may not want to share the same interests with your partner because you want to be with someone who is different and can introduce you to new things.

- *What values must my partner have?* Something that may be very certain to you are your partner's morals and values. You may want to be with someone who possesses the same type of values you have in your life. Morals and values are crucial for any relationship because you want to make sure the people you date are on the same page as you. Sharing these values will bring you closer together.

At the end of the day, you're not trying to look for someone who is the exact same as you. You merely want to be with someone who you can relate to on a deeper level. Sometimes it's valuable to be with someone who doesn't share all the same values and interests as you, because then you can view and experience life from another perspective.

General Things to Look For

If you're struggling to find things to look for in a partner, you can look for qualities that will be great to find for any partner. You may be someone who doesn't care about specific qualities, characteristics, and interests, so you just choose anyone to date. Just because you don't have specific qualities you look for in a partner doesn't mean you should just date anyone. These are some general positive qualities you should look for in any person you date:

- **Honesty and trustworthiness.** A relationship can't work if there isn't honesty and trust, because this will just cause continuous conflict that will ultimately result in your relationship's demise. This is why it's crucial to find someone who is honest and easy to trust. This will make your relationship healthy, as you're able to trust what your partner has to say. You don't want to be constantly wondering and worrying about what your partner is doing.

- **Emotional maturity.** It's impossible to find someone with no emotional baggage or issues at all, but if you find someone who is emotionally mature, this is someone who is a great option to date. Someone who has emotional maturity will be able to be the bigger person during moments of conflict. They will also be able to admit when they're in the wrong and make it up to you. Dating someone with emotional maturity will help you to have a healthy relationship, as they will have a sense of calm and understanding about them. They will also be more empathetic and loving toward you.

- **Affection.** Whether we like to admit it or not, we all crave affection from our relationships. Being with someone affectionate will ensure that you have enough intimacy that makes your relationship fulfilling. You want to look for someone who uses a similar love language as you and shows affection in this manner. If they show affection differently, this doesn't mean you should write them off because they can always grow and adapt for you. As long as they are willing to show you affection, that's all that matters.

- **Independence.** Although you will want a partner who cares about you and is sensitive and affectionate toward you, you need to have someone who displays balance. It's so important to pursue a partner who is independent because if you find someone who wants to be dependent on you, you will find that they become too clingy and needy. Being in this type of relationship will drain you and take a toll on your relationship. You want to be with someone who has their own life and can live without you. Someone who is too dependent is a major red flag that you should look out for.

There are many other positive qualities that you can look for in a partner. If you're looking for a long-term, meaningful relationship, you must ensure that you pursue these positive qualities. You want to be with someone who will make your life better and more enjoyable, not someone who will cause problems in your life.

Don't Limit Yourself Too Much

Although it's important for you to have an idea of what you want from your partner, you mustn't limit yourself too much. If you strictly only look for someone with certain requirements, you will overlook potential partners who could be great for you. When you limit yourself, you miss opportunities to find someone who may be perfect for you, so you must be open minded.

When you're finding the right person for yourself, the main thing you should look for is whether they're a good person or not. You don't have to focus on the specific qualities of each person, but rather, just put emphasis on whether they will be good to you and fit your lifestyle.

Consider Your Compatibility

When you're looking for someone to date, you shouldn't only consider the facts like the interests and passions you share, because you also need to consider something that you can only feel. You need to think about your compatibility with the potential partners you meet. Sometimes you meet someone who doesn't seem like they would be a suitable partner for you on paper, but you have great compatibility in person that builds a strong connection. This is why it's valuable to consider your compatibility when you meet someone.

Do You Click?

You may experience a date where you just click with someone instantly. You may not have a lot in common and they don't inhibit all the qualities you desire, but you still click together. Considering whether you click is more than just ticking characteristics off of a list; it's about forming a special bond or connection with the person you're dating. To consider whether you clicked with your date, you can ask yourself the following questions after the date:

- *Do you feel a spark?* You meet your partner, go in for a hug, and maintain eye contact with them; in that moment, you feel bubbling emotions within you. If you feel this spark with the person you're on a date with, it's a sign that you connect instantly. Having an undeniable connection with someone is very obvious. Even if you're a bit shy with each other at first, you can feel the spark between you.

- *Does conversation just roll?* When you're on a date with someone you click with, you will find that conversation just rolls effortlessly between the two of you. They're so easy to talk to and you can talk about absolutely anything. Although you may not have the most in common, you never run out of conversation together. You can joke around and have fun together like you've known each other for a long time.

- *Do I have to think about it?* Lastly, you should ask yourself whether you need to think about whether you have a click with your partner or not. If this is something you have to put a lot of thought into, then you probably didn't click with your date. It is usually quite obvious when you have an instant connection with someone.

Although having this spark and compatibility with someone is important, it's not everything. Sometimes you can feel a strong connection, but it is only motivated by lust and not love.

Putting Yourself Out There

If you're trying to look for the perfect partner for you, you're not going to find it by staying home and avoiding interactions. You need to be able to put yourself out there in order to get the right partner for yourself. You may be struggling to find the right partner for your life because you don't know how to put yourself out there to meet someone who's perfect for you. These are just a few ways you can put yourself out there better.

Try Dating Apps

In the society we live in today, it's become extremely easy for you to date and meet new people. In the past, it was a lot more challenging to find new people to meet and date, but due to social media, you can connect to an infinite amount of people that you wouldn't have in real life.

There are so many different dating sites available out there that can be used to find different types of partners. There are dating apps that help you to find someone who is looking for a serious long-term relationship, as well as dating apps for people who are looking for casual dating relationships. Whatever type of relationship you're looking for, there's a dating app that can connect you to people who are looking for the same things as you.

When using a dating app, you must be cautious because it's not always as successful and safe as people may think. You're essentially meeting strangers off of the internet, which means that you could go on dates with people who are unsafe. You may also find that the person you pursue on a dating app is a catfish, as they pretend to be someone they aren't over the phone. So, when you use dating apps, it's important to proceed with caution and low expectations.

Shoot Your Shot

Sometimes you just need to gain courage to shoot your shot when you're interested in someone. We can meet people in life who take our breath away, but we feel too scared to approach them because we have a fear of being rejected. These are some things you can consider when you're trying to shoot your shot with someone you're interested in:

- **Ask yourself what's the worst that could happen.** The biggest thing that may deter you from approaching someone you're interested in is the fear of rejection. You feel like it's going to be the worst, most uncomfortable experience ever, which prevents you from ever shooting your shot. This is why you should ask yourself what's the worst that can happen to you. Yes, you may be rejected, but it's not going to kill you or harm you in any way. The worst that can happen is that they're not interested and you move on with your day.

- **Have a unique pickup line.** If you want to shoot your shot with someone in person, you better have a good line to grab their attention. If you just say "hello" or "how are you," you're not going to make a good enough impression. Think of something unique to approach them with so that you can really pique their interest. This will not only make them feel more inclined to engage in conversation with you, but it will also help them to remember you in the long run.

- **Know when to back off.** When you shoot your shot with someone, you must know when it's time to give someone their space. You can't be overbearing when you tell someone you aren't interested. Unfortunately, that's the risk of shooting your shot, as you may approach people who have zero interest in you. If the person you approach tells you they're in a relationship, then you should back off and wish them a good day. If you notice that they are uncomfortable or they don't want to talk to you, then you need to take that social que and give them some space.

There's nothing wrong with shooting your shot with people who you're attracted to and interested in; you never know what it could turn into. But, you must avoid approaching every attractive person you see because you don't want to be known as that kind of person. You must also avoid forcing interactions with everyone because this will just make you unappealing to a potential partner or date.

Make the First Move

If you have a secret crush on your friend or acquaintance, but you've kept this to yourself, it's time to tell them how you feel. If you know this person is in a relationship or they're not interested in dating, then you might as well cut your losses and avoid having this awkward conversation. But, if you know there's a possibility they may like you back, then why not make the first move?

There are many instances where friends turn into married couples because they've built a healthy foundation for their relationships. Make the first move in these relationships because you never know what could happen for you. Your relationship may flourish into something beautiful.

Ask Your Friends to Set You Up

Nobody knows you better than your friends, so if you're struggling to find a suitable partner for yourself, your friends can set you up with someone perfect for you. If you approach the right friends who have the best intentions for you, they can choose someone for you to date. That's a real catch. If you're afraid to ask your friends to set you up, these are some ways you can go about doing it successfully:

- **Don't be shy.** At the end of the day, if you're approaching real friends who care about you, you should never be afraid to make this request. Your friends know you well and they want you to be happy, so don't be surprised if they're filled with excitement knowing they get to set you up with someone. Once your friends find someone for you to go on a date with, you mustn't be shy then, because it's your duty to go on that date. Don't let your nerves get to you because you never know what could come from this date.

- **Let them know your requirements.** Just because your friends are choosing someone for you to go on a date with doesn't mean you should have no say in it. You want your friends to find someone who's actually suitable for you because then this exercise will be worthwhile. So, don't be afraid to offer your requirements that are crucial for you in a relationship. This will help them to find someone suitable for you, but you mustn't be too rigid and strict with requirements.

- **Don't be too pushy.** Although you may have to go out of your way to ask your friends and may even have to remind them every now and then, you must know when you've reached your limit. It's okay to remind your friends every now and then, but continuously asking them about it will make them feel less interested in helping you. Your friends have their own problems to deal with, so don't dump your love life on them. They will help you if they actually want to and if they have the time for it.

Your friends helping you to find a partner may be exactly what you need to get out of your comfort zone. They may have a better understanding of what type of person you need, especially if you're constantly chasing the toxic partners. You may find that they pick dates that you click with well and it can turn into something more. If your friends don't find your soulmate, at least you will have a better understanding of what you want in a partner.

Be Open to Opportunities

You may be reading this book wondering why you can't get into a relationship, but anytime someone approaches you, asks for your number, or asks you out, you turn them down immediately. You need to be open to the dating opportunities that are presented to you because they could be exactly what you need to fill your life with love!

These are some ways you can be more open to dating opportunities:

- **Get out of your comfort zone.** Staying in your comfort zone is where love goes to die. It's impossible for you to find someone you can spend the rest of your life with if you're constantly staying in your comfort zone. You need to be able to do things, go places, and open yourself up to experiences that may take you out of your comfort zone. This will provide you with the opportunity to meet dates who are perfect for you.

- **Say "yes" when you're asked out.** If you're ever asked out by someone, instead of being nervous and turning them down, take the opportunity to do something different. It can seem illogical to go out on a date with someone who you don't even know, but you never know the connection you could form with them. When you do this, it's important to go on a date in a public setting so that you don't put yourself in danger.

- **Be open minded.** Ultimately, when you're approaching dating in your life, you need to be able to have an open mind. When you get asked out by someone you're not attracted to, or you feel like you have a small spark with someone you've been best friends with for ages; it's important to have an open mind in moments like these. That will help you to embark on a love story that may be unexpected, but completely satisfying. Don't close yourself off to any options, unless you know they will be bad for you.

There are so many dating opportunities in front of us that we don't even realize at times. In order to attract the love you want in your life, you need to be open to many opportunities. You may find an unexpected partner who fulfills your life. When you keep yourself open to opportunities of love, this is when you will find the right partner who makes you happy!

Avoid the Toxic Ones

Last, but not least, you need to be able to avoid dating the toxic individuals who scream red flags. Yes, it's important to keep your options and ideas open so that you can experience the opportunity to fall in love. However, it's also crucial for you to keep yourself aware and cautious. The dating scene can be extremely harsh and hurtful if you're not careful.

You need to make sure that you're looking for the right partner who's on the same page as you, as well as someone who has good intentions for you. You need to avoid going for the toxic type who you know will end up hurting you. Although they may look like a fun date or partner, this situation will probably end in tears.

If you struggle to determine if someone is toxic, then fear not. Later on in this book I will show you how to identify when someone has red flags and you'll learn how to avoid them on your dating journey. You deserve a partner or date who actually cares about you.

Chapter 7:

Building Healthy Relationships

If you're getting back into the dating world, it's crucial for you to work toward building healthy relationships. Although using seduction, hypnosis, and telepathy are effective ways for you to date, you need to be able to find ways to build healthy relationships. When you know how to build healthy relationships, they will last long, as well as leave you feeling fulfilled and content.

Having a healthy romantic relationship can transform your life and fill you with long lasting love. When you chase empty and meaningless relationships, that feeling of happiness fizzles away in seconds. Being in a healthy, strong relationship will not only last long, but it will provide you with comfort and belongingness.

The Importance of Healthy Relationships

We all need healthy relationships in our lives that make us feel content and fulfilled. Whether these are friendships or romantic relationships, it's all valuable to us. If you are looking for a more long-term and long lasting relationship, it's crucial for you to have a healthy relationship with your romantic partner.

Having a Comfortable Relationship

One of the biggest benefits of having a healthy relationship is that you develop a really comfortable relationship with your partner. Being in a comfortable relationship means that you don't experience insecurities within your relationship, trust issues, and extreme conflict or turmoil. This means you have a peaceful relationship that brings you fulfillment and true happiness. Having a comfortable relationship will benefit you in the following ways:

- **Reduced relationship stress.** When you're in a comfortable and healthy relationship, you will notice that your stress is drastically reduced. This is because both you and your partner never put each other in positions to hurt or upset one another. Being in a toxic relationship with no trust and lots of issues can be a continuous stress in your life. Your relationship shouldn't be something that causes stress in your life, if anything, it should provide you with the opposite. Being with a healthy partner can help you to reduce other stressors in your life, as you have a partner to help you tackle all of your scary problems.

- **Having a greater sense of purpose.** A true long lasting and healthy relationship provides you with a greater sense of purpose that fills you with long-term happiness. You feel fulfilled in your life because you have someone to build a life with that is filled with purpose. You may want to get married and have children with this partner, which will bring a greater purpose to your life.

- **Better and healthier lifestyle.** Being in a healthy relationship doesn't only help you to have a healthier love life, as it also helps you to live a holistically healthier life. When you're with the right person who is a healthy influence on you, you will begin to strive for a healthier, happier lifestyle. You may find that you are fitter, eat healthier foods, and have greater confidence and love for yourself. Your partner becomes a positive influence in your life and your love for each other motivates you to be the best version of yourself.

You'll never understand the true benefits of a healthy relationship until you find yourself in one. Being in a healthy and comfortable relationship can make you so happy and content with your life. You never have to stress and worry about whether you're enough for your partner. However, before you're able to be in a healthy relationship, you need to know what is required of you to be in one and how you can improve yourself to be the best partner possible.

How to Have a Healthy Relationship

You may be wondering to yourself how you can go about having a healthy and meaningful relationship, especially if you're used to having casual relationships or toxic ones. You may think being in a healthy relationship is dependent on the person you're with, but this is not the only thing that makes a healthy and happy relationship.

How to Improve Yourself

When you're trying to be in a healthy relationship, it's not just about finding the right partner who isn't toxic, or learning how to be in a relationship. It's also about working on yourself. Something that's not spoken about enough is that working on yourself is crucial if you want to be in a healthy, long-lasting relationship. Although we may not like to face reality, none of us are perfect, which means that we need to work through some of our personal issues in order to be a more suitable partner for a healthy relationship.

Be Your Own Individual

Being in a relationship can sometimes make you forget about your identity, and this is one of the worst things you can do in a relationship. When you find yourself being too dependent on your partner to the point where you forget about your own true essence, you need to do some work to rediscover yourself and who you are. Being your own independent individual is important if you want to have a healthy relationship. These are some ways you can find yourself if you feel lost within your relationship.

Spend Time by Yourself

If you're trying to find yourself in a relationship, you can't always be smothered by your partner. Although you may love to spend all of your time with your partner, it's important for you to spend some time apart so that you can rediscover your individual identity. If your partner isn't on the same page as you and doesn't want to spend time apart, then you can do the following:

- **Do it alone while together.** A great way to pressure autonomy while still staying connected with your partner is by doing things alone while you're together. You may be together physically, but you're both participating and focusing on your own activities that bring you joy.

- **Have your own dates.** You and your partner may have had countless dates together, so why not suggest going on separate dates by yourself? You can both go on individual dates that you've always wanted to do or you can go on individual dates that you've done together. For example, you can have a date night alone by going to your favorite restaurant you frequently visit together.

- **Participate in your favorite activities alone.** When you're in a relationship, you don't have to do everything together. You can tell your partner that you can do both of your favorite activities alone. For example, you may love doing pottery, so you can go to a class by yourself, while your partner enjoys playing games online which they can do on their own.

It's important for you to have that quality time with yourself. Doing this will help you remind you that you are an independent individual with your own thoughts, desires, and personality.

Take Care of Other Life Relationships

If your relationship with your boyfriend, girlfriend, husband, or wife is the only relationship that has any real meaning in your life, then you're in trouble. It's okay to prioritize this relationship because it's valuable to you, but you mustn't neglect your other life relationships because you're so focused on your romantic partner.

Consider the other relationships in your life, whether they're family members, work-related, or friendships. Determine whether you give these relationships the attention that they deserve. Maybe you've been guilty of ignoring your friends because you've been putting all of your focus into your relationship. Just because you're pursuing a romantic relationship, this doesn't mean you must neglect the other relationships in your life.

Take time to care for your other relationships so that you remain with these important bonds. You will also find that spending time with other people whom you love and care about will give you space from your partner to find yourself. You become reconnected to your original roots, which helps you to find your true nature again.

Don't Control Your Partner

When you're trying to work on finding yourself in a relationship, you need to be able to give your partner the same amount of space to achieve this. You never know if this is something that your partner is struggling with as well. It's more common than you think for both partners in the relationship to lose themselves in that relationship, especially when it's a very needy and intense one.

When you find yourself trying to instruct your partner and tell them what to do, take a second to perform the following mindfulness activity. It's composed of three questions that will help you to conclude whether you're being too controlling over your partner at the moment or not. To practice this short exercise, you must ask yourself the following questions:

1. ***What tone and wording am I using?*** The first question you should ask yourself is about your tone and choice of words. Being controlling can cause you to talk in a demanding and overpowering tone, which can be intimidating for your partner. If you use words that don't suggest your partner should do something, but rather commands them that they have to do it, then it can showcase that you may be controlling at that moment. Although your request may not be controlling or harmful

to your partner, the way it comes across may seem intimidating.

2. ***Is this something I want?*** To determine whether you're trying to control your partner to do something you want, you should ask yourself whether this is something you want or if it's what your partner actually wants. Ultimately, you should be supporting what your partner wants, instead of instructing them to fulfill what you desire. However, it's important to recognize that sometimes what you want is good for them. It's relative to the context of the situation.

3. ***Will it be valuable for my partner?*** If you are commanding your partner to do something you want, you simply need to ask yourself one question to determine where it's controlling or not: "will it be valuable to my partner?". Sometimes as a loved one, you have to command your partner to do things they don't want to do so that they can do what's valuable for them in the long run. If your request adds value and growth to their life, it may be just what they need, and you're looking out for them, instead of being controlling.

You need to think to yourself if you're controlling in any way in the relationship. If you are, you shouldn't beat yourself up for being too overbearing, but you should instead work toward being more hands off. Let your partner have space to do things on their own and make their own decisions. You may find that doing this allows them to be less controlling in return, which ultimately helps you to work on finding yourself more.

Work on Self-Love

Before you embark on a journey to fall in love with another person, you need to be able to fall in love with yourself. Can you genuinely look at yourself and think that you love yourself? For many of us, loving ourselves can be challenging, and this is something that needs to be worked on before getting into a serious relationship.

It's really challenging to be in a healthy relationship if you don't have self-love or confidence in yourself. You will find that this lack of self-respect and care will result in you becoming a problem in your relationship. You may become jealous, distrusting, overwhelmingly negative, as well as dependent and needy. This is why it's so important for you to love yourself before you jump into any relationship. These are some steps that will help you to work on self-love:

1. **Stop comparing yourself to others.** Before you get into the habit of showering yourself with self-love and care, you need to stop yourself from filling your mind with self-doubt. If you continuously put yourself down, you will never be able to truly love yourself. One way to stop self-doubt is by preventing yourself from making toxic comparisons. You need to stop comparing yourself to people you're jealous of, because that will only cause self-hate. The only person you can compare yourself to is you!

2. **Be easy on yourself.** The next way you can prevent self-doubt is by being easy on yourself. Although you may think it's good to have extremely high standards for yourself and to strive to be a perfectionist, it can actually be really toxic for your self-worth. Unfortunately, you are a human, which means that you come with flaws and mistakes. You need to be easy on yourself when you make mistakes and fail, because being too hard on yourself will only break down your confidence.

3. **Embrace your strengths and weaknesses.** Whether you like to admit it or not, we all have strengths and

weaknesses that make us unique individuals. We need to embrace both our strengths and our weaknesses so that we can become the best version of ourselves. Get a notepad and write down all of the strengths that you think you have. You can ask friends and family or think about your skills and interests. Then, after considering your strengths, take some time to write down all of your weaknesses.

4. **Take on risks and opportunities.** Being able to trust yourself to make the right decisions will help you to find more confidence within yourself. You need to take risks in life and embrace opportunities so that you can prove to yourself that you are worthy. You'll be pleasantly surprised to find that you excel and do well. This will make you love yourself for accomplishing all the things you didn't think you could!

5. **Get rid of negative voices.** Lastly, you must get rid of the negative voices that make you doubt yourself. This means that you need to get rid of the negative self-talk that you participate in. Whenever you find yourself being harsh and rude to yourself, replace these negative words with something kind and positive. You also need to get rid of external negative voices that are stunting your self-love growth. If you have people in your life who bring you down, there's no space for them when you're trying to love yourself, so get rid of them or ignore what they have to say!

Self-Improvement Activity

If you're really struggling to improve yourself to the point where you're a good partner to date, then it's valuable to try out the next practical activity. You can use this simple activity to determine how good of a partner you are at the moment or what type of partner you would be if you got into a relationship. From this, you can discover where you can improve upon yourself. To practice this exercise, you should get out a journal or a piece of paper so that you can answer some questions that will help you to learn more about yourself as a partner. These are the questions:

- *What kind of partner am I?* When you consider this question, you must keep in mind your common behavior in a relationship and the way in which you've treated your ex-partners. If you are a more relaxed and casual partner, this will make for a healthy relationship; but if you're an intensely jealous partner, you're bound to experience problems.

- *What toxic behavior do I display?* This is the question that nobody likes to answer, but it's crucial if you want to find yourself in a healthy relationship. Being aware of the toxic behavior you're guilty of in your relationship will help you to know what is required of you to improve yourself.

- *How do I feel about myself in a relationship?* The most important question for you to ask yourself is how you feel about yourself when you're in a relationship. If you feel happy and secure in a relationship, it's a sign that you're ready for a healthy relationship. However, if you feel insecure, jealous, and self-conscious, it's a sign you need to work on loving yourself before you pursue a relationship.

Once you answer these questions, you'll have a better idea of what type of person you are in a relationship. This will make you aware of your negative aspects that may make you a toxic partner. From this, you will have a better idea of what you need to do to work on self-improvement in order to be a better partner. Doing this will help you to continue this activity by writing down practical ways you can work on yourself.

Managing Conflict

One of the keys to having a healthy relationship is being able to healthily manage conflict between you and your partner. Take a second to consider how you react and behave in conflict. Are you someone who is cool, calm, and collected, who chooses to handle the conflict at hand in a rational manner; or do you find yourself getting triggered and reacting irrationally? Although we like to think of ourselves as the calm reactors, it can be challenging to keep your calm when you're having an argument with your partner.

Unfortunately, no matter how healthy you may be as a couple, it's impossible to get rid of conflict altogether. You're bound to experience conflict in your relationship that can be frustrating, but you do have control over how you respond and manage your conflict. If you find a healthy approach to conflict in your relationship, you will find that it won't be an obstacle in your life anymore.

You and Your Partner Against the Issue

A common mistake people make when they find themselves in conflict with their partner is that they behave like they're going against each other. Having a fight with the person you love shouldn't mean that there's tension between the two of you. When you and your partner get into an argument, you need to change your mindset. Instead of getting angry with each other, you should acknowledge that the issue is between you and the problem.

When you have this mindset, it helps you to be less angry toward each other, as you realize that you aren't each other's enemies. The problem at hand is the issue you're facing, and you should both work on tackling the problem together. This will help to bring you together, instead of making you push each other away.

Stay Calm

When you are in conflict with your partner, it's important for you to be able to manage your emotions because you don't want to let your anger and frustrations get the better of you. If you struggle to stay calm when you're experiencing conflict with your partner, then you need to find exercises that can help you to calm down. These are some tips that will help you to cool off in an argument with your partner:

- **Step away for a bit.** If you feel yourself getting really heated up and frustrated at the moment, it may be a good idea to step away from the conflict for a bit. If you are too worked up at the moment, you will never have a productive conversation with your partner. You will find that you both get worked up and end up endlessly blaming each other. Taking some time to yourself can make you realize where you may have been wrong. This can help you to come back to your partner and have a calm and rational conversation to resolve the conflict.

- **Practice breathing.** Working on your breathing is a very effective way for you to calm yourself down. It may sound silly that breathing can calm you down, but working on your breathing can truly help you to calm your nerves. Sometimes all you need to calm yourself down is to take a deep breath in and out. This will help you to center yourself so that you can slow down your thoughts, settle your emotions, and feel overall calmer.

- **Be mindful of your words.** When you're in an argument, it can be easy to get upset and say something you don't really mean. You may find that an argument turns into you and your partner getting upset with other things that have nothing to do with the original issue because of how you've been reacting and behaving during the conflict. When you find yourself angry, be mindful of your words, and if you feel like you're going to say something you'll regret later, then choose to be more quiet in the moment.

Being able to calm yourself during an argument is crucial because emotions can make things a lot more intense than they need to be. When you calm down, you're able to approach this conflict of interest with a more clear mind. This helps you and your partner to approach the issue together, instead of making enemies of each other.

Chapter 8:

Avoid Red Flags

Whether you're trying to seek healthy, long-lasting relationships, or you're looking for a short-term fling that makes you happy, you need to be able to avoid red flags. Red flags can be seen as warning signs in a person that should signify you to avoid this individual. If you want the dating experience to be a fun one, you need to be able to identify when someone is displaying too many red flags so that you can avoid them by all means.

What Are Red Flags?

We've all been in a relationship that has hundreds of obvious red flags that should deter us from that specific individual, but we often choose to ignore them. Red flags are signs of toxic behavior that your partner or date may display. They can either be really discrete or extremely obvious. It's important to notice really bad red flags earlier on in the relationship so that it doesn't end up hurting you in the long run.

Red flags aren't necessarily all forms of toxic behavior, because we all have a few toxic habits that aren't deal breakers in a relationship. What you need to look out for with any individual that you date are big red flags that will result in a toxic, unhealthy relationship where you get hurt or mistreated.

These are the main types of red flags you want to avoid that can be detrimental to you in the long run:

- **Narcissism.** You may not think narcissism is a major issue in someone, but when it comes to a relationship, it can provide lots of unwanted obstacles. When people are narcissistic, they care only about themselves. This can make them controlling, selfish, and egotistical. From this, you will find that they treat you horribly, get jealous easily, and try to control your life.

- **Victimization.** If you're with a partner who is constantly playing the victim, you'll get tired of it really quickly. Someone who is always playing the victim is someone who can't take accountability for when they're wrong at times. When you find yourself in conflict because they did something wrong, they will always spin it around and make you seem guilty. These types of partners can be very manipulative, as they indulge in guilt-trips and drain you emotionally.

- **Aggression.** Of course, one of the biggest red flags you have to look out for are any signs of aggression. If you're with a man or woman who shows aggressive and violent behavior, you need to run the other way. If they have intense anger issues when you start dating, this is a sign that they may be physically or verbally abusive down the line once you get more comfortable in the relationship. If your partner physically hurts you in any way, you need to look after yourself and leave the relationship.

Unfortunately, there are many individuals who are great at hiding their red flags, especially in the beginning of the relationship. This is why it's important for you to find any signs and patterns of behavior that could showcase toxic red flags. These are just a few types of dangerous partners to look out for, and although they may not seem harmful in the honeymoon stage of your relationship, they can end up ruining your life or idea of love in the long run.

How to Notice Red Flags

You may be the type of person who always sees the good in people first. You are less aware of their negative aspects because you focus on their good side. Although it's important to value the good aspects of people, you shouldn't ignore red flags, especially when they are potentially harmful to your happiness. There are various types of red flags out there, but these are just a few common red flags that you should keep a lookout for:

1. **Constant put downs.** Does your partner ever try to put you down verbally by projecting negative comments on you? Do they make you feel self-conscious with their constant insults? Having a partner who puts you down verbally is a major red flag you need to avoid. You should have a partner who lifts you up and makes you feel confident in yourself, instead of having someone being nasty to you always.

2. **Intense jealousy.** Everyone gets a little jealous every once and a while, especially when their love is feeling threatened. But, if you're in a relationship with an insanely jealous partner, you must know that the relationship will not end well. If your partner doesn't trust you, even though you have given them no reason to be distrusting, then it's a red flag you can't miss. You may think it's cute in the beginning, but this jealousy can transform into something a lot more threatening.

3. **Never wanting to compromise.** In a healthy relationship, it's all about compromising at times. You or your partner can't always have their way in life, so you need to be able to compromise when you aren't on the same page. If your partner refuses to compromise because they always want things to go their way, this is a massive red flag. Being in this type of relationship will become draining because your partner always has to win or be in the right.

It's so important to identify the red flags in the people you date, because this can save you from getting hurt. You may be finding it difficult to see any negatives in your partner because you see them so highly. These are some tips that will help you have better luck at finding the red flags your partner displays:

- **Take off the rose tinted glasses.** To see the toxic behavior your date or partner may display, you need to be able to take off the rose tinted glasses that make you see everything positively. When you're in love, you may not see any negatives in the person you're with, but you need to be realistic and consider whether your partner has any red flags you must steer clear of.

- **Look for patterns.** The best way to determine whether your partner has toxic and harmful behavior is by taking a look at patterns you may have noticed. We all have our moments of weakness where we aren't the best partners, but if it becomes a pattern, then this is something deeper that should be looked at.

- **Ask friends and family.** Sometimes it can be impossible to see the negatives in the people we love, especially when you're falling in love with a special someone. This is why it's valuable to ask your friends and family members to give their unbiased opinion. They may see some toxic behavior from an external point of view that you wouldn't notice within your relationship, because you were blinded by love.

Being able to notice red flags in the dating stage or earlier stages of your relationship will help you to avoid a hurtful future with this individual. No one wants to experience a toxic relationship that makes them question love.

Analyzing People

If you want to learn how you can avoid the wrong type of person and introduce the right person in your life without harmful red flags, you should analyze your dates. Being able to analyze whether someone is toxic or good for you, is a valuable skill to have when you start dating. It will help you to become a good judge of character. These steps will help you to read people better:

1. **Create a baseline.** Each individual has their own habits or quirks that make them unique. Find out what they do that makes them different, for example, they may touch their nose every time they genuinely laugh.

2. **Find inconsistencies.** Once you know this person's common behavior, you can notice when they deviate from it. For example, if they laugh without touching their nose, you can tell that they are being fake toward you.

3. **Look for patterns.** Noticing just one outlying behavior doesn't mean much because we all stray away from our norm every now and then, but if you find a different pattern of behavior then you'll be able to tell if they're being their true self around you.

4. **Notice personality ques.** Once you put all of this information together regarding your date's behavior,

you're able to have a better understanding of their personality. You can also identify how they feel about you through the connection between their introverted or extroverted personality and their habits. For example, if they have shy and awkward habits when they're a more extroverted person, it may be a sign that they're interested in you and it makes them nervous.

If you analyze a date you're really interested in and your skills help you to discover that they're not the right one for you, then you need to be able to practice discipline. You may be really attracted to or interested in this person, but you need to be self-disciplined so that you attract the right people into your life.

Do You Have Red Flags?

You should also consider whether you show any red flags as a partner. When you're so busy looking for red flags in the individuals you're dating, you forget the toxic traits and behavior you may be displaying on your end. None of us are perfect, so it's important for us to determine the red flags we may be showcasing to the people we date.

How to Determine if You Have Red Flags

It's easier to identify red flags in other people than within ourselves. To discover whether you display red flags to the people you date or not, you need to be honest and transparent with yourself. This may not be enjoyable because you have to recognize some unfavorable qualities about yourself, but you need to delve into the negative aspects of yourself if you want to become the best version of yourself.

These are some examples of red flags that you should look for in yourself:

- **You're too needy.** There's nothing wrong with feeling really close and connected to the person you're dating, but the problem starts when you find yourself being too needy toward them. Your neediness makes them feel guilty for not dedicating all of their time and energy to you. You may do things that make you overly possessive and unhealthy, which can take a negative toll on the relationship.

- **You're unable to listen.** None of us are perfect in life, and that isn't a red flag. You're bound to have negative aspects of yourself, but this shouldn't be alarming to the people you date. A red flag is when you're unable to listen to the person you're dating and admit when you're wrong. If your partner is upset with something you've done or said and they're trying to communicate how they feel, you should listen openly. If you don't actively listen to them and undermine everything they say, this is a massive red flag.

- **You don't deal with personal issues.** One of the biggest red flags you may have is being unable to deal with your personal issues. It's important to acknowledge the negative aspects of ourselves because this will help us to work toward growth and self-development. If you can never accept when you're wrong in a situation and you shift the blame on your partner, it's a sign that you don't know how to be self-reflective and you don't work on your personal issues.

- **You can't handle not getting what you want.** Sometimes in life, you won't get exactly what you want and that's okay. If you get offended and upset because you don't get what you want, that's a toxic trait. In life, we all have turns to get what we want, so it's unfair to always expect to get everything you desire from your partner. A relationship is all about compromising, so at times you need to make the sacrifice to compromise what you want to make the person you're dating happy.

It's vital to remember that having a few manageable red flags isn't the end of the world, as we're all bound to have a few harmless negative traits. The problem is when you have too many red flags, or if you have red flags that could be harmful for a relationship. You don't have to get comfortable with your toxic habits, as you can train yourself to get rid of them. If you've identified negative traits like these within yourself, it's time to utilize the following steps to eliminate them:

1. **Accept your toxic traits.** Before anything else, you need to take time to accept all of your flaws, no matter how bad they may be. We all need to take a long hard look at ourselves in the mirror and come to terms with the negative sides of ourselves. Once you truly accept yourself for your red flags, you'll be able to work toward eliminating them. It's impossible to get rid of these toxic traits when you hate yourself for them. You need to be accepting in order to truly conquer your flaws.

2. **Recognize your triggers.** If you want to eliminate your toxic traits and behavior, you need to be able to determine where these red flags begin. You must ask yourself, "What triggers this behavior?". There's always something that can catalyze our worst qualities. For example, if you're a needy person and your partner says they have to go on a work trip without you, this can trigger you to be needy and possessive. Once you discover what triggers your red flags, you're able to get to the root of the issue.

3. **Start small with changes.** When it comes to unlearning your toxic habits, it'll take time for you to actually see change. Unfortunately, it's impossible for you to see the changes you may want overnight. This is why it's important to take baby steps toward change. Merely being aware of your red flags can help you to take measures to prevent yourself from being toxic. A small change you can make to become less toxic is stopping yourself in your tracks. For example, you may find that your red flag is being overly judgmental. When you find yourself about to say something judgmental, you can stop yourself from saying it out loud. Although it's a small step, doing it frequently will help you see incredible results over time.

4. **Make a plan.** It can feel impossible to change the habits you've grown so accustomed to. The best way to tackle this is by making a field plan with achievable goals that you work toward on a daily basis. Having a set plan can help you find practical strategies to approach your red flags. You can make a long-term plan that you want to follow, and you can set daily goals for yourself. For example, each day you can set a new goal that will help you to combat your red flag. If your red flag is being self-absorbed, one day your goal could be to only talk about yourself twice in that day. Another goal for a different day may be to ask the people in your lives about their days, to show interest in them.

5. **Ask for help.** It can be challenging to tackle your negative characteristics, so you can ensure that you aren't going through this change on your own. Asking people who you care about to be there for you and help you to stay accountable will keep you in line. Your friends and family can alert you when you're showcasing red flags and this will help you to stay aware of your behavior. You can even alert the people you date by being upfront

about your red flags. This may be seen as admirable to your dates as you're being honest. They can also help you to be a better person, by making you aware of when you're displaying red flags.

When we take time to practice self-awareness, we mustn't be ignorant to our problems. Unfortunately, we aren't perfect, as there are aspects to ourselves that can make us toxic partners. When you get into a relationship, you bring your emotional baggage with you, so it's your job to work on making your baggage more manageable for your potential partners. Work on your red flags, so that you can find a partner who is worthy of your love.

Activities to Avoid Red Flags

If you're struggling to identify red flags in the people you date, and if you can't identify whether you're displaying red flags, you may want to find other ways to be more aware of red flags. Sometimes toxic red flags can be disguised really well, so you never find them until it's too late. Or, you may find that you cause problems in all the relationships you're in because of your red flags. These next two activities will help you to prevent these two case scenarios from occurring.

The Toxic Checklist - Avoiding Red Flags in Others

When you're falling in love with someone, getting closer, and building a bond with them, it can be so challenging to see things clearly. You think this person you're dating is perfect because of all the good moments you experience together. This can make you avoid the bright red flags that are waving in your face.

For this activity, you will learn how to use this toxic checklist to avoid toxic individuals who could become a potential threat to your happiness and quality of life in the long run. The following is a long list of qualities of a toxic person in the beginning stages of a relationship. You must tick off each discrete toxic trait that you've noticed in your partner:

- They joke about you cheating on them or leaving them.

- They keep you away from your family and friends.

- You feel more insecure than usual.

- They only talk about themselves and how they feel.

- They don't ask about you and your feelings, or even ask, "how was your day?"

- They are always interrupting you in conversation and telling you that you're wrong.

- You feel desperate for approval and care.

- They are constantly providing you with "constructive criticism."

- You don't feel like yourself with them and they bring out the worst in you.

- They compare you to their exes.

- They're constantly blaming other people for their problems.

- They feel like they have to compete with you.

- Your partner doesn't remember things that are important to you.

- Your relationship starts to feel like work.

Once you've finished this checklist for the person you're dating, you may have a better idea of what you're dealing with. If you've ticked off nothing, then you may have a keeper in your hands, and if you've ticked off a few of them, then there probably isn't anything too concerning that you should worry about.

However, if you have more than six of these toxic traits ticked, then it may be a sign that this individual will not be a great fit for you. Although these signs may not seem that toxic, in the long run, once you're both settled, their behavior will escalate to something more harmful.

Use this checklist as a guide to help you, but don't be impulsive to leave your partner if they fail the test. It's important to start off with conversation to see if they're willing to change and improve for you. If you notice that there's no change and that their promises were empty, you know that you deserve better!

Journaling Activity - Eliminating Your Red Flags

For this activity, you can work toward discovering your own red flags so that you can eliminate your toxic behavior in relationships. After trying out all the tips previously mentioned, you may still be struggling to see the negativity within yourself. This quick and easy journaling activity may be just what you need to find accountability for your red flags.

All you need to do is get a journal so that you can answer the following important questions:

- *What have my exes criticized me for?* You need to consider some of the things you've been criticized for in your past relationships or dates, because they may show you a pattern that you weren't aware of. If one of your exes told you this, it may not be reliable information, but if it was a common statement that you received from all of your exes, it's an indicator that it's a red flag of yours.

- *What are my biggest weaknesses?* You can then proceed to ask yourself what some of your weaknesses are that can be harmful to your partner in a relationship. Even if your weaknesses negatively impact you, you may find that they turn you into a partner who can be toxic and harmful. For example, your weakness may be that you're insecure in yourself, which causes you to become overly jealous when it comes to anyone your partner is friends with.

- *Can I admit when I'm wrong?* An important question to ask yourself is whether you're able to admit when you're wrong. Although you may have red flags, are you able to admit that you have them and strive toward improving them? If you want to be in a healthy relationship, you need to be able to own up to your wrongdoings so that you can be a better person to be in a relationship with.

Once you answer these questions, you'll have a better idea of whether you have bad red flags or not. You may discover that you've actually been self-sabotaging all the relationships you've been in. Coming to this realization will help you to finally move forward as a better partner. Once you know what your red flags are, you'll find it easier to work toward being in a healthier relationship.

Chapter 9:

Improving Communication Skills

Another way you can work on improving your relationships and dating life is by transforming your communication skills. How you communicate with people on dates makes a big impact on how well your relationship forms. It's normal to struggle with communication, especially if you're a less extroverted individual. This chapter will help you to become a better communicator.

The Impact of Communication on Your Love Life

You may not realize how important effective communication skills are for your love life until you properly explore dating and relationships. You will realize that you need to put extra effort into your communication so you can use it to improve your connections. Effective communication will have countless benefits for your love life, whether you're dating people or you're in a relationship. These are just a few benefits you may experience from effective communication in your love life:

- **Building trust.** When you're in the beginning stages of dating someone, communication is a lot more important than you realize. If you want this person to become your romantic partner one day, you need to use healthy communication in the beginning of your dating relationship. When they see that you're an open and honest communicator, it builds trust, which makes them more open to dating you. Being an open communicator will make your partner feel more secure in the relationship, as they trust you more.

- **Learning more about each other.** Effective communication can also help you to learn more about the people you date. It's impossible to learn more about the person you date if you don't have the conversations that help you to learn more about them. Asking questions, bringing up different topics, and listening to what your date has to say can teach you so much about them. Learning more about each other can help you to grow your connection with each other.

- **Avoiding miscommunications.** Having effective communication will also help you to avoid miscommunications and conflict between you and your partner. You put all of your opinions and thoughts out there so that you can be truly understood. Conflict occurs when people don't understand each other, and the only way to alleviate this issue is by communicating with clarity. Less conflict results in a healthier, happier relationship.

Your communication with your date and potential partners determines whether your love life is successful or not. If you aren't mindful of your communication, you may end up passing up a date or relationship that may be perfect for you. You need to be able to communicate to connect and build a relationship with someone, so once you have your communication skills conquered, you're able to build the love life you desire!

How to Be a Better Communicator on Dates

You may find that you struggle to communicate effectively when you're on dates because your nerves get the best of you. If you struggle to start a conversation or keep a conversation going when you're on a date with someone, it's important to develop your communication skills. You want to be able to have conversations effortlessly so that you can get to know the people you date, as well as give off a great and confident first impression.

Utilize Small Talk

Many people have a misunderstanding of how useful small talk can really be. They just view it as something awkward that can only make a conversation less successful. What people don't realize is that small talk, when used effectively, can turn a conversation from dry and boring, to deep and meaningful. It can act as the foundation of communication because it can get your conversation started. These are some effective ways in which you can utilize small talk to improve your conversations with dates:

- **Don't be boring.** Small talk is unsuccessful when you become a bore. Don't talk to your date about the weather or boring topics like this, because it will make your date totally disengage from the conversation. You need to be original and unique with your small talk, as it will intrigue your date and make them more interested in conversation with you.

- **Think of personal topics.** When you're on a date with someone, your objective is to dig deeper with them. You want to learn about their personal life and experiences, and to discover this information, you need to bring up the right topics. However, when you bring up personal topics, it's important to not be too intrusive and overbearing. You want to respect your date's personal space, so if they don't want to talk about something, then don't be shy about changing the topic.

- **Build on from the small talk.** Your small talk shouldn't just end at generic conversation, as you need to build onto it. You are able to create meaningful conversation from small talk, so don't remain in the bounds of surface level communication. Use your small talk topics to proceed with deeper conversation. Once you start a conversation with small talk, you'll be able to branch off the conversation onto something more meaningful, so don't be afraid to dig deep.

Small talk can be just what you need to start conversations with your dates. When you feel as though you don't know how to approach conversation with the person you're on a date with and you don't know much about them, utilizing small talk successfully can help you to learn so much about them!

Conversation Starters

If small talk isn't for you, then you can find a way to use conversation starters to get communication going between you and your date. If you're feeling anxious about going on a date because you don't know what to say to get a decent conversation started, as well as you don't know what to say once the conversation begins to get dry and awkward, then preparing a few conversation starters will help you immensely.

Having some prepared topics that are interesting to you will get a conversation flowing again. These are just a few conversation starters that will help you in any awkward moment during a date:

- **Your most desirable travel destinations.** For most of us, traveling is something that excites us. Talk to your date about dream travel destinations you want to visit, and you may end up discovering a more adventurous side to your date.

- **Your goals and ambitions in life.** When you want to connect with your date on a deeper level, it's valuable to start talking about your goals and ambitions in life. This will help them to learn that you're a motivated person who wants to be something in life. It will also influence them to share their life ambitions.

- **Your favorite movie or book.** Sometimes a conversation with your partner doesn't have to be deep for you to connect. You may find that simply talking about your favorite book or movie gets the both of you excited.

- **The important people in your life.** A great conversation starter that can give someone a greater insight into your life is the topic of important people in your life. When you tell your date about the different important people in your life, they learn a bit more about you and you discover more in return when they share the people that are important in their life.

Conversation starters provide you with the opportunity to talk about things you care about, which helps you to learn the right things about your date. This is why it's valuable to come up with these conversation starters before your date so that you feel prepared to connect with them.

Ask Questions

When in doubt, ask questions. Asking the right questions is the best way to save any conversation you're having on a date. There are so many reasons why utilizing questions effectively can be beneficial to you. Firstly, it can help to fill in the awkward silences when the conversation runs out. It's a great way to ensure you and your date have more of an opportunity to connect, as you speak more.

Secondly, asking questions on a date can be valuable because it shows that you're interested in what your date has to say. You want to show your date that you have a genuine interest in your conversation and their opinions, so make them feel included and special by asking them the right questions.

Questions are the perfect way to get the conversation rolling, as they're one of the best ways to discover more information. When you ask questions, you learn. Think about the type of information you want to discover from your date so that you can come up with questions that help you to retrieve this information. Having suitable and interesting questions will be the best way to keep a date vibrant and intriguing.

Utilizing Effective Body Language

When we think about communicating to make a good first impression on a date, we often focus on the words we say and how we deliver them. Something that can often be overlooked but is influential to your effective communication is body language. The way you use your body as you talk makes a big impact on how people receive what you have to say.

- **Use flirtatious body language.** If you want to seduce, attract, and make a great impression on your date, you can make the most of your body language by being flirtatious! You may be thinking to yourself that you don't have the sex appeal to pull off this non-verbal communication, but you will be surprised to discover how easy it is to be flirtatious with your body language. You can use this type of body language by maintaining flirtatious eye contact with your date. You can touch them casually on the shoulder or arm when you're talking to them. These are all small cues that you're flirting with your date.

- **Have open and welcoming body language.** Did you know that your body language can make someone feel either welcome or unwelcome when talking to you? If you're standing with your arms folded and your body facing away from your date, it gives a non-verbal impression that you're uninterested in them. However, if you face them, have an open body posture, and use hand gestures, it makes the person you're on the date with feel more welcomed by you. You want to be more welcoming so that your date feels comfortable and interested in return!

- **Reading your date's body language.** Not only can you use body language to communicate effectively, but you can also determine how your date is feeling by reading their body language. Whether we realize it or not, we all use specific body language when we feel a certain way. You're able to tell how your date is feeling about you and your time together by considering their subconscious body language. If your date is smiling, laughing, and has

119

a very open body language, you can assume that they are enjoying the date. But, if their facial expression looks bored and uninterested, and they're facing away from you with their arms crossed, it's a sign that they're less interested in you.

You already use body language in your day-to-day life without even realizing it. You can now use body language to your advantage by being more aware of what you're doing. You are able to stop yourself from using shy and closed off mannerisms, so you can give off the right confident and welcoming impression to your partner. You'll also be able to use your body language to make the mood of your date more romantic and flirtatious.

How to Read Body Language

Body language plays a big role in your dating life, as you can use it to get closer to a potential partner. You need to understand your date or partner's body language in order to portray empathetic and psychic abilities. Being able to gather how your date is feeling through their body language shows that you're an empath who can identify the following body language signs:

- **Study the eyes.** When you're trying to read the body language of your date, you want to start off by studying the eyes. It's true when they say that the eyes are the window to the soul, because they can tell you everything a person is feeling or thinking. Although their facial expression may be telling you one thing, their eyes will reflect the truth of their internal thoughts and emotions.

- **Focus on the face.** When you hear body language, you may feel as though you need to focus on the physical body of your date, however, you can get a lot of information from facial expressions. You must look for things such as your date touching their face because they're shy and giddy around you. Or, if they have crows feet by their eyes while they laugh or smile, you're able to tell that it's genuine.

- **Notice their feet.** Did you know that the position of someone's feet can let you know how they feel about you? This is why it's valuable for you to look at your date's feet as they speak to you. If your date's feet are faced openly toward you, it's a sign that they feel open and interested in you. If their feet are facing away, they could be disinterested in your conversation.

Communication Don'ts

At the end of the day, you should communicate with your date in a way that makes you feel most comfortable. The key to great communication is being confident and going with the flow. The previous tips will merely help you to get through a conversation with ease, especially if you're experiencing nerves. Although you should feel comfortable to communicate freely, there are still some communication no-nos that you should consider. These are just a few don'ts you should keep in mind while dating:

- **Don't interrogate your date.** Yes, it is important to ask questions on a date, which we established earlier, but it's important not to get carried away by asking too many questions. You need to have a healthy amount of questions that help to boost your conversation, rather than just bombarding your date with question after question. You may find that you ask too many questions when your date gives you very brief responses and they don't ask you anything in return. The best way to deal with this situation is by relating to the answers you get, rather than making your date a Q&A.

- **Don't invade your date's personal space.** Although using romantic and flirtatious body language is valuable, you definitely need to know your boundaries. It may be a romantic date you're on, but you don't know whether the person you're on a date with is comfortable with being touched or not. You need to test the waters to see how your date feels about you being close to them and touching them. If they reciprocate your energy and share the same body language, that's a good sign to continue. However, if you can see from the body language that they may be uncomfortable, it's time to give your date some personal space.

- **Don't talk about something your date is uncomfortable with.** When you're learning about someone for the first time, you're going to want to talk about every topic possible. Anything that comes to your mind, you'll want to bring it up so that you can learn more about your date. Although it's great to bring up any topic, there are topics that may make your date uncomfortable. You'll never know what topic makes your date uncomfortable until you bring it up. If you notice them becoming quiet, cringing, or looking uncomfortable, then take a mental note that this isn't a topic you should bring up again.

- **Don't overthink it.** Overthinking should be your biggest enemy when it comes to communicating. If you're too busy spending your time worrying about what you're going to say on your date, you'll end up communicating unsuccessfully. You'll freeze up, stutter, and struggle to improve the conversation between you and your date. Your communication is supposed to be an enjoyable experience, so you should consider how to do it successfully and then let your conversations flow naturally.

It may seem like this is a painfully long list of rules for communicating on a date, but when you think about it, it really isn't that restrictive. Communication is subjective to each person, because what you may find enjoyable may not have the same sentiment for the next person. As long as you're giving your date space to communicate back and you're making them comfortable, then that's what matters the most!

Examples of Effective Dating Communication

You may understand a bit more about how communication plays a big role in your dating life, but you're unsure of how you can practically apply this knowledge to your love life. Actively learning how to communicate better can be challenging, so here are some examples that can help you to conquer your dating obstacles or worries.

Example 1 - Breaking Awkward Silences

Your date started off on a good note, but conversation is starting to fade. You don't know what to say to break this awkward silence, as it feels like ages since you've said anything to each other. In this example, you will see how you can break awkward silences with the right conversation starters and small talk.

You: The menu looks nice.

Your date: Yes, I like this place a lot.

You: Then I'm glad we're here.

Your date: Me too.

Silence

You: If you had to choose a favorite meal, what would it be?

Your date: That's a very difficult decision, but I think I would have to go with lasagna. What about you?

You: I'm a huge burger guy. You can never go wrong with a burger and fries. Well, that's not entirely true, actually. I went to this one restaurant and I ordered a beef burger and the meat was basically still bleeding. When I complained, they said that's how it's supposed to be. I don't know how people eat raw red meat.

Your date: Same! It all looks so unappealing to me. I like my food well-cooked, to the point where it's a little burnt.

You: That's funny, because I feel the same way!

This example conversation went from dry and awkward, to enjoyable and fun. At first, you were both engaging in unsuccessful small talk, as you were being very limited with your replies and statements. Once you brought up your conversation starter about which meal is your favorite, conversation started flowing. You even added a personal story which helped you to bond over something, as well as lighten the mood of your conversation.

Example 2 - Including Your Date

You may find that you're on a date with someone who is very reserved and quiet. You end up talking a lot about yourself but you want to ensure they feel included in the conversation. In this example, you can see how to include your date, especially if they're not talkative.

You: For my job, I essentially oversee everything that leaves the office. You can imagine that this is an extremely demanding job, as I have to be aware of everything happening around me. It's just extremely exhausting, so by the time the weekend comes, I just want to stay home and binge-watch my favorite TV shows.

Your date: I get you. I feel-

You: This is literally the first date I've been on in such a long time because I never have the energy to socialize or leave the house.

Your date: Yeah.

You: I'm sorry. I feel like I'm just talking about myself. Please tell me about your work—what do you do on a daily basis? I'd love to hear more about it.

Your date: Thank you. I'm actually a baker, so most of my day consists of me standing, mixing, and waiting.

You: Haha, that sounds fun. But do you enjoy what you do and is it your passion in life?

Your date: It really is my passion, even though I complain sometimes. My dream is to open up my own bakery one day!

You: Wow, that's amazing!

This example of how to communicate on a date shows you how you can redeem a conversation when it becomes one-sided. You may begin to talk too much about yourself, which also causes you to interrupt your date when they speak. We all have moments when we get like this, and the best way to recover is by asking your date questions. By turning the conversation back to your date, they were able to feel included in the conversation again. You proceeded to ask follow-up questions which resulted in you learning about what your date's passions are.

How to Be a Better Communicator in a Relationship

Having effective communication skills isn't just important for your dates, as it's also crucial when you're in a relationship. You need to learn how to communicate with your partner effectively. Having a healthy and happy relationship is impossible if you don't have effective communication with your partner.

Be Open and Honest

When you're in a relationship, it's critical for you to be an honest communicator. When you bring lies and dishonest communication into a relationship, it's a recipe for disaster. This is why honesty and truth are the foundation of any healthy relationship, because without them, there will be never-ending relationship issues. This is how you can be a more honest and open communicator:

- **Avoid telling lies.** A healthy relationship is one where no lies are told. When you tell lies to your partner, you may think you'll never get caught, but lies have the habit of catching up with you in the long run. Even if these are merely white lies that you're telling, it's important to prevent yourself from getting caught up in this habit because once you tell one white lie, you will get into a routine of telling them frequently.

- **Tell the truth.** Being in a relationship means that you need to tell the truth even when you don't want to. Hiding the truth is just as dishonest as telling a lie, so it's important to tell your partner what they would want to know. Sometimes it can be scary to be honest because you don't want to disappoint or hurt your partner, but it's important to know that if they found out on their own and your secret was revealed, they would be hurt a lot more. So, opt instead to be open and honest, no matter how bad it may be, because the truth has a way of revealing itself.

- **Be clear with what you say.** If there's something you need to get off your chest about how you feel, it's crucial to be clear when you communicate it. Too often we feel shy expressing something personal or negative, so we end up beating around the bush. Doing this will only confuse your partner, so you need to be open and straightforward. This will help them to understand the point you're bringing forward, and it will help you to get closer together.

If the foundation of your relationship is built on honesty, then you are going to have a long and successful relationship together. It's also important to be open and honest with your partner when you do something detrimental to the relationship. You must be honest, even if you don't want to date your partner anymore, so that you don't end up wasting each other's time when you're unhappy.

Listening to Your Partner

Being in a healthy relationship means that you and your partner need to listen to each other. If you're constantly talking about yourself and you're not actively listening to what your partner has to say, you end up missing their point of view. You need to be able to listen to each other if you want a long-lasting relationship with healthy communication.

If you struggle to listen attentively when your partner is talking, you can use the three As, which stands for the following:

- **Attitude.** You need to start off your listening with a positive attitude. When you listen to your partner with negativity, judgment, and a negative attitude, you will never truly be able to understand what they're telling you from their perspective. You need to have a positive and open attitude when you're listening to your partner, so you can listen to them with an open mind. This will help you to understand their perspective, as well as make you listen with empathy, rather than listening to criticism.

- **Attention.** Of course, the most important thing to prioritize when you're listening is to pay attention to what your partner is saying. When you listen to your partner speak, are you merely just hearing what they say and letting your mind wander onto other topics? If this is you, you need to work on being a more attentive listener. You need to be able to actively listen to what your partner is saying so that you can respond suitably. Paying attention to the details of their words and their tone will help you to have effective conversations that mean a lot to your partner.

- **Adjustment.** As with the first A, for this A, you need to be able to listen with a more open mind. When you're listening to your partner to give your opinion, encouragement, or your perspective, you need to be able to adjust how you usually think. Communicating openly helps you to see things from a different perspective, so you need to be able to adjust your responses to suit this perspective.

Be honest with yourself. You don't like it when other people don't listen to you when you speak, so it's important to show your partner that you're actually listening to them. The more you attentively listen to your partner, the more you will learn about them and your relationship as a whole.

Couple Communication Exercises

You may find that the biggest issue in your relationship is that you and your partner have a barrier between you, which makes it challenging to communicate. You find yourself constantly butting heads with each other because you're not on the same page, and you also struggle to understand each other's perspective.

The only way to solve this tension between you and your partner is by working toward having healthier and more effective communication together. You may use all of the tips and tricks that have been provided to you, but this may not be enough to improve your communication. Remember that communication is a two person activity, so both you and your partner need to work on it together.

This makes it valuable for you and your partner to acknowledge your communication issues so that you can engage in practical activities together. Practicing communication exercises with your partner will help you to improve your communication, which will ultimately influence your bond together to strengthen it.

Mirroring Technique

You may find that there's tension between you and your partner because your partner thinks that you're not actually listening to them when they talk, or vice versa. When either of you are talking about something important to you, the only response you get in return is "uh-huh" or a nod of the head. Although this is meant to signify that you're listening, sometimes it can come across as though you don't care.

This is where the mirroring technique comes into play. Either you could make use of it, or you could make your partner aware of it. It's an extremely simple and effective technique that can help you to appear more attentive and caring to your partner. Appearing more involved in what your partner is saying will improve your communication immensely, as your partner will want to open up to you more. You will experience less conflict and get closer as a couple, because it's always heartwarming knowing your partner is listening to all of your problems, successes, and verbal thoughts.

To practice this technique, you simply mirror what your partner is saying. If your partner is telling a story about work, complaining about something that happened, or voicing their true feelings, you should repeat back some of the things they say. For example, if they say, "Then Vicky told me that I was lying to her and hiding something at work," you can then reply, "Really? She said you were lying?" Something as small as this shows that you're listening and following the story.

When you mirror your partner, ensure that it's organic. You want to actually listen to what your partner is saying, not just repeating them to get away with not listening. You also shouldn't mirror too frequently, because this could appear suspicious or annoying to your partner. It's all about finding the right balance that comes off naturally for you.

Gratitude Exercise

We can often get so comfortable in our relationships that we fail to communicate our appreciation for one another. You may find this is something that has happened in your relationship, especially if you've been together for a long time. To have a healthy, loving relationship, it's crucial to show your partner how grateful you are for them in your life.

This is why it's valuable to practice this gratitude exercise, especially if you feel like you haven't been appreciative of your partner. This gratitude exercise can be practiced in many ways, so choose a style that works best for you and your partner. Here is a basic step-by-step guide that you can follow to show and receive gratitude with your partner:

1. **Sit your partner down and be open.** Before you get started with this exercise, you need to have time with your partner to discuss where you are as a couple. If you need to practice this activity, then there has probably been a lack of appreciation and love between you. Communicate to your partner that you want to feel more loved and appreciated, as well as that you want to practice being more loving toward them. Once you're on the same page, you can get started with this gratitude exercise.

2. **You each say two things you love about each other.** Take a look at your partner and think of two things that you love about them. One thing should be related to their personality and behavior, and the other thing can be related to their physical or sexual attributes. Remember that your partner also wants to be appreciated physically

and sexually, because this keeps passion alive. After you say the two things you love, ask your partner to express the two things they love about you.

3. **You each express what makes you grateful for each other.** Next, you can express to your partner something you're grateful for them doing. In a relationship, we do so much for our partners without even recognizing it, so now is the time to make your partner feel appreciated for everything they do. No matter how big or small their actions are, your partner will be happy to feel appreciated. For example, you may be grateful for how much cooking and cleaning they do around the house. After you tell your partner what you're grateful for, ask them what they are grateful for when it comes to you!

4. **You both say something to show each other how important you both are.** Whether we like to admit it or not, we all like to feel special and loved. You may say that you don't care about it, but feeling important to someone can provide you with the best feelings ever. This is why it's important to end off this activity by showing each other how special you both are to each other. Tell your partner something unique about them that makes them stand out in your life. For example, you can tell them how they're your best friend because they make you laugh nonstop.

For this activity to work, you both need to be actively spreading love and gratitude to each other. It won't work if it's one-sided, so you must ensure your partner wants to participate in this activity as much as you. Practicing this activity frequently will have a great impact on your relationship, as you will eventually get into the habit of expressing your gratitude and appreciation without this exercise.

The Sandwich Method

One of the most challenging things to communicate with your partner are negative feelings and opinions. You want to voice how you feel about something, but you don't want to end up offending your partner in the process. The sandwich method can help you to say something negative in the best way possible so that your partner receives it well.

This method is easy to use, as all you need to do is sandwich your negative statement into two positive statements. Think of two positive things to say to your partner which showcases your love and care for them, say one of them first, then provide your negative statement, and end off with another positive statement.

For example, if you're unhappy with how your partner cooks food because it's borderline inedible, then you can start off by saying, "I'm so grateful for all of the work you do around the house," you can then provide your negative statement; "But, I have to be honest with you. Your food hasn't been great lately." After saying this, you can end it off with another positive statement such as, "I know you're so busy with work and building an amazing career for yourself, so I was wondering if I can do more of the cooking to lighten your load?"

Although you broke some negative news to your partner, you said it in a way that made you sound understanding and caring, instead of being judgmental and hurtful. By offering to lighten your partner's load to cook, it shows that you care more about them than the food they make.

At the end of the day, it's important to be open to criticism in a relationship. You may not want to hear anything negative about yourself and your behavior, but being open to what your partner says can make you a better person to date. However, when you deliver constructive criticism, you will find that it's valuable to use this sandwich method to soften the blow.

Chapter 10:

Learning Emotional Intelligence

If you want to find the right partner, have a healthy relationship, and become a dating master, learning emotional intelligence is a crucial skill. Being more emotionally intelligent helps you to be more sensitive and empathetic to the individuals you date. Having a better understanding of your emotions will make you a better partner, and being more understanding and aware of other people's emotions will allow you to become insightful and empathetic.

The Importance of Emotional Intelligence in Love

There are countless reasons why emotional intelligence is important in a relationship. These are just a few of them:

- **You are self-aware.** Having emotional intelligence helps you to be more self-aware of your own emotions. We all have emotions and they can be really detrimental to our relationships if we don't work toward understanding and regulating them. When you're self-aware of your emotions, you're able to manage how you behave, which means you become less reactive and aware of your partner's feelings.

- **You become more empathetic.** When we get caught up in our emotions, it can be easy to only consider our own perspective. This makes us neglect what our partner may be feeling because we're focused on ourselves. When you become more emotionally intelligent, your perspective opens up, as you become empathetic to the needs and feelings of your partner. You're able to see things from their perspective more, which makes you more empathetic.

- **You are able to set boundaries.** One of the main reasons for emotional intelligence in a relationship is being able to set healthy boundaries with your partner. Something that isn't spoken about enough is that being in a relationship means you need boundaries for certain things. There are certain behaviors, actions, and words that may make you uncomfortable, so you'll want to set boundaries to ensure you're both happy.

- **You understand your partner more.** Having a high EQ means that you understand how your partner is feeling more. You understand emotions and why people feel the way that they do. This means that you have a deeper connection with your partner where you understand each other emotionally. You will find that this reduces conflict between you.

Have You Found "The One"?

When you become more emotionally intelligent, it can even help you to determine whether you've found "the one" or not. You may not believe the concept of having a soulmate is real, but it is true that there are more suitable individuals to date that may be the perfect match for you. If you're trying to find this special person who makes you feel complete, you need to use your emotional intelligence to determine whether they're "the one" or not.

Consider Your Feelings

To determine whether someone is the right fit for you, you need to start by considering your feelings toward them, as well as the feelings you have when you're around them. What you feel can tell you a lot about how connected you are to them. You may think that because you have feelings of love toward them that they may be perfect, but "the one" will make you feel a lot more emotions than just love. These are a few feelings you can expect when you find the perfect partner:

- **You feel like you want to love and protect your partner.** If you have this feeling that makes you want to love and protect your partner deeply, then it's a sign that you have found someone special. You won't feel like protecting and taking care of just any person you date, as you will only feel this way for someone who feels precious to you.

- **You feel content and satisfied with your relationship.** Being with someone can make you feel really content and in love. True love gives you a feeling of satisfaction and comfort because you know it will last long and keep you happy and content. If a relationship brings you constant stress, emotional turmoil, and sadness; it's a sign that you're in the wrong relationship and that that person isn't "the one" for you.

- **You don't just feel lust for your partner.** Think about the person you're dating and consider what feelings you have about them. If you just love them for the way they look physically and other superficial qualities, they may not be "the one"; however, if you find yourself loving absolutely everything about them, you may be on the right path. When you find this person, you end up loving both the smallest and biggest things about them, even their weaknesses. You love the way they smile and laugh, and you're in love with their charming personality.

- **You are positive and caring toward others.** Not only does the right person make you positive and caring toward them in the relationship, but it also makes you a loving person toward others. You will find that you start caring about others more and your love intensifies for the people in your life. This makes you a great person to be around because you are positive and friendly!

How Your Life Has Been Impacted

True love doesn't only impact how you feel; it also has an influence on your external life. Being with the right person can influence you to have a better life, so when you're with someone you're falling in love with, you should consider the different ways they may be impacting your life.

These are three things that you can consider that will aid you in discovering whether you're with a suitable partner or not:

1. **Excelling in your career.** Have you noticed that you've been doing extremely well in your career? You're more confident, so you've been taking opportunities and risks that have been paying off. You've also been more of a team player, which has made your boss notice you more. Excelling in your career is a sign that you're with the right

partner. They motivate you to do well in your career, as well as make you more confident in yourself, which rubs off on your work.

2. **Being a better friend.** Dating "the one" doesn't only help you to become a better partner toward them, but it also makes you a better friend to the people in your life. If you notice yourself growing distant with your friends, it may be a sign that you're not in the right relationship, especially if your partner is purposely keeping you away from your friends and family. However, if you become a better friend and family member, it's a sign that you're in a loving and special relationship, and the people in your life will notice this as well!

3. **Looking after your overall health.** Being with "the one" also motivates you to be the best version of yourself both physically and mentally. You feel inclined to look after your well-being because you want to be healthy for your partner. You eat healthier, exercise frequently, and work on bettering yourself mentally. Holistically, this will make you a happier and healthier individual.

If you notice this change of success, well-being, and happiness in your life, it could be a sign that you're on the right track. If your quality of life improves drastically while this partner comes into your life, it's a sign that they should stick around for longer!

What You Need vs What You Want

Determining whether someone is the one for you or not can be quite challenging, especially if you have lots of options that you enjoy spending time with. It can feel impossible to find "the one" when you don't know what's best for you and which type of person will make you happiest in the long run. To have better success determining who's the one for you, you can try out the following simple activity.

This exercise will help you to distinguish between what you want and need in a relationship, as we can often get the two mixed up. When you truly desire something, it can make you feel as though this is something you need, but in reality, it may not be the best thing for you. For this exercise, all you need is a piece of paper to figure out what type of person "the one" will be. To fulfill this activity, follow these steps:

1. **Make a list.** You start off this activity by making a list of everything you think you need in a partner and in a relationship. Think about all of the qualities in a person that you've always thought were important in a potential partner. For example, you need them to be funny, caring, protective, emotionally open, or physically active. You can list about 10 characteristics or requirements that you've always deemed important to you.

2. **How does it make you feel?** After you make the list, you now need to consider how these qualities actually make you feel. For each characteristic, you must ask yourself two questions. The first question must be, "does this characteristic in a partner make me feel energized or calm, or does it cause me emotional turmoil?" You must then ask yourself, "does this quality in a partner make me feel pleasant, neutral, or unpleasant?" For example, the characteristics could be protective, energized and excited, and pleasant. You must present each one of the characteristics like this.

3. **Consider your answers.** Once you've got it all written down, you can evaluate these feelings to determine whether it's what you need or want. Feelings of lust or desire are what we want in life, but they don't provide us with what we need. These desirable feelings are often

superficial and short-term, whereas the deep, meaningful love we need in our lives is more long-term and sustainable. If you wrote down that a characteristic makes you feel pleasant and energized, it's a sign that this is something you want. On the other hand, if you wrote down that a characteristic makes you feel calm, pleasant, or neutral, this signifies that it's something you need because it will bring peace and comfort into your life!

After practicing this activity, you should have a better idea of what you actually need from a relationship. This may transform what you thought your idea of the perfect partner is. But you'll end up with the idea of someone who can add real value to your life.

Understanding Intuition

When you awaken the empath within you, you will realize a lot more about yourself. Your gut can tell you more about love than you may recognize. When you are in touch with your intuitive side, it can help you pursue the right people, as well as amplify the empath within you and your psychic abilities.

We all have intuition, whether we're aware of it or not. It's your job to get more in touch with this side of yourself, so you can be more knowledgeable when you approach relationships. Following your intuition is all about trusting yourself. When you make decisions, you can practice using your intuition by trusting your gut instinct. If your mind is telling you that the person you're on a date with might be "the one," listen to your gut because it's most likely leading you in the right direction.

How to Enhance Your Intuition

Our subconscious and psychic minds sometimes know what's best for us more than our conscious minds do, so it's valuable for you to listen to that persistent voice in your head. You may struggle to follow your intuition because you aren't in tune with your psychic abilities or empath characteristics. These practical tips can help you to enhance your intuition:

- **Listen to that persistent voice.** Do you have a voice or thought in your head that just won't disappear? When your gut is trying to tell you something, it can often repeat itself in your mind to emphasize what's right for you. If you experience this persistent voice, it's crucial for you to follow your intuition.

- **Keep a clear mind.** When you're trying to make an important decision in your love life and you don't know what your intuition is trying to tell you, you should take a deep breath in and out so that you can clear your head.

- **Awaken hidden powers.** You may be struggling to follow your intuition because you're out of touch with your internal powers. We all have these internal mental powers, whether we are in touch with them or not. To get in tune with this psychic empath side, you'll need to spend some quiet time trying to connect to your deeper side. You can accomplish this by meditating, journaling, or practicing deep thinking so that you can get in touch with your more powerful side.

How to Be More Emotionally Intelligent

Some of us are more emotionally intelligent than others, so practicing emotions may come easy to you. On the other hand, it may be something you struggle to learn because it's not something you've ever learned or used actively. Just because it's something you're not used to doesn't mean you won't be able to develop emotional intelligence. It's a skill and way of thinking that you can adapt to with practice. These are some practical activities that will help you to embrace emotional intelligence.

Activity 1 - The Four Rs

If you want to develop some emotional intelligence skills, then this is an activity for you. By developing these traits, you will find it easier to be more emotionally intelligent in your relationships. These four Rs represent characteristics that can help you to better your emotional intelligence skills:

- **Recognition** - Being able to recognize the emotions you experience is crucial, as it's the first step to bettering yourself. If you don't identify the emotions within you, you won't be able to handle the emotions of your partner. When you feel yourself experiencing intense emotions that are influencing negative behavior, take a second to identify the negative emotions you're using. If you can recognize what emotions you're feeling and what they make you feel, it'll help you to tackle them.

- **Regulation** - When you identify your emotions, you know what you're dealing with at the moment. From this, you need to work on regulating your emotions. It's not enough to simply know what you're feeling because you also need to know how to regulate the emotions you feel. If you don't know how to regulate your anger, you may end up lashing out on others verbally and physically. This is why regulation is a crucial skill for your emotional intelligence because you become aware of the emotions you're feeling but you don't let them overwhelm you.

- **Reading signals** - Although emotional intelligence is about focusing on your own emotions so that you understand yourself on an emotional level, it's also about understanding other people emotionally. When you have a better perception and understanding of other peoples' emotions, especially your romantic partners, it can improve your relationships drastically. Your partner will show signs when they're unhappy about something, so it's important to pick up on these cues.

- **Responding** - Learning how to respond to your own emotions and the emotions of others is important. Firstly, you need to be able to respond to your partner in a regulated manner, as established earlier. If you're upset with something your partner does or says, you must respond maturely. You also need to be mindful of how you respond to your partner when you see that they're upset. Sometimes the best way to respond to negative emotions from your partner is by being comforting.

This isn't necessarily an activity you can follow, so much as it's a state of mind you should learn to adapt to. If you want to be more in touch with your emotional intelligence, you need to be able to integrate these four Rs into your everyday life. The following two activities will help you to find practical ways to reflect emotional intelligence in your relationship or dates.

Activity 2 - Identifying Your Emotions

Being able to identify your emotions is easier said than done, especially if you don't have experience understanding and interpreting the different ways you feel. For this activity, you can discover how to practically identify your emotions when you feel yourself being overwhelmed. Following these steps can help you to determine what emotions you're experiencing and what might have triggered them:

1. **Pay attention to your physical sensations.** When you experience a strong emotional reaction, it is often accompanied by physical sensations. Feeling anxious, depressed, negative, or even really positive emotions can trigger physical sensations that you can be more aware of. You may struggle to identify the different emotional feelings you experience, so it may be easier for you to observe your physical sensations that feel different than usual. For example, you may breathe differently, have sweaty palms, or feel tense physically.

2. **Observe your feelings.** Once you identify a change in your physical sensations because of how you're feeling, it's time to observe your feelings and what they may be. You may find it easy to determine when you're feeling happy or sad, but if you want to develop emotional intelligence, you need to be able to observe your feelings in greater detail. If you feel sad, you must consider what type of sadness you're experiencing. Are you lonely, regretful, depressed, or grieving? All these emotions have distinct differences between them.

3. **Identify your emotional triggers.** After discovering what emotions you're experiencing, you can take some time to identify what's triggering these emotions. Although you may not be aware of it, your intense

emotions are always going to be triggered by something. Being able to determine what these triggers are cannot only help you to manage how you feel, but it can give you greater insight on what you need to work on to improve managing your emotions in the future.

Activity 3 - Responding Over Reacting

When you find yourself frustrated by what someone says or does to you, it can be easy to go into reaction mode because you want to give your date or partner a piece of your mind. Although you're entitled to feel the way you do, it's important for you to respond to this person in a calm and mature manner. You can let someone know how you really feel without reacting aggressively and making matters worse. Follow these steps in your relationship so that you can learn how to respond to your partner instead of just react:

1. **Take a deep breath in and out.** When emotions are intense and you're feeling annoyed or overwhelmed, it's crucial for you to take a beat before you respond to your partner. If you respond in the heat of the moment, you may find yourself reacting by saying something you'll regret in the long run. Being calm and taking a second to think will help you to respond in a mature and rational manner, which means you stand up for yourself and say what's on your mind, without being offensive.

2. **Think before you speak.** When you're feeling emotionally overwhelmed, it's important to think before any words come out of your mouth. Sometimes when we're in the moment of intense emotions, our words can be nasty and hurtful. This is why it's crucial for you to think about your words before you say them out loud. Consider whether what you're going to say is a rational

and fair response, or if it's a rude and unnecessary reaction. This will stop you from saying anything you may regret in the long run.

3. **Communicate assertively.** Just because you need to stop yourself from reacting negatively to your partner, doesn't mean that you should keep your opinions to yourself. If you're upset about something, then you can communicate it assertively and confidently to show how serious you feel about a certain topic. When you communicate this calmly with assertiveness, people are more likely to take you seriously.

If you use this quick exercise every time you feel your emotions arise, it will help you to relax and respond in a calm and rational manner, instead of reacting in a way that would negatively impact your relationship. Frequently practicing how to think before you speak will help you avoid any conflict or issues further down the line.

What to Do if Your Partner Has Low Emotional Intelligence

Although you may be working toward being more emotionally intelligent, your partner may not be on the same path as you. If you notice that your partner is less emotionally intelligent than you, this is not the end of the world. You can work with your partner to create a deeper, more understanding emotional connection together. This will help you to not only connect on a deeper level, but it also helps your partner to realize what you need from your relationship emotionally.

These tips will help to ensure that you and your partner are on the same page:

- **Communicate your wants and needs clearly.** If your partner is less emotionally intelligent, then they may not have a clear idea of what you want from them. Although you may communicate what you require emotionally, they may not get the right idea. This is why it's crucial for you to communicate with clarity and specifics.

- **Send "I feel" messages.** If you want to emphasize how you feel to your partner, it's valuable to use the words "I feel" when you're trying to get your point across. You don't want to accuse your partner of doing things wrong, because this will turn into a finger pointing contest where you and your partner are against each other. When you emphasize that this is how you feel, then you and your partner can conquer how you feel together.

- **Have discussions on dates.** When you have a less empathetic and emotionally intelligent partner, you need to have the necessary conversations. If you're an emotional person or you're in touch with the emotional side of yourself and your relationship, your partner probably doesn't understand how you feel because they haven't experienced it themselves. This is why you need to have open discussions to explain your perspective and mindset. This will help your partner understand how to communicate with you while being mindful of both of your emotional sides.

Although your partner may not prioritize emotional intelligence in your relationship, it doesn't mean that it's not important. You need to put in the work emotionally so that you and your partner can have a deeper connection on every level. You will find that nurturing the emotional aspects of your relationship will result in far less conflict together, as you approach issues rationally.

Conclusion

We all deserve a love life that brings us happiness and fulfillment. After reading this book, you may have a better idea of what you're looking for in your love life. Although you may desire and want a specific partner, this may not be what you actually need in your life.

The best way for you to approach dating successfully is by having an open mind when you enter this new world. Things may be really different from what you're used to, but this doesn't mean you're too outdated for dating. Having an open mind as you try out Tinder and social media dates can help you to get connected to the perfect partner who brings you happiness.

At the end of the day, your dating objective should be to find someone who makes you feel happy and ultimately improves your quality of life. You need to avoid dates with people who are walking red flags and display toxic behavior, because they won't be good for you in the long run. Although they may provide you with a sense of thrill in the moment, they could end up hurting you, which will put you off dating altogether.

Although there are bad people out there who have the wrong intentions, this doesn't mean you must close your heart off to the opportunity of falling in love. If you have a guarded heart, it will prevent you from fully embracing your dates, so you need to be willing to put yourself out there fully.

You are bound to find someone suitable for you and what you desire for your love life. You deserve that type of love in your life that makes you feel satisfied and complete, so don't be afraid to look for it!

A Message From the Author

Thank you for reading and/or listening to this book.

If you enjoyed it and found it helpful for you and your love life, please leave a review on the site where you purchased it.

Your feedback is valuable to me and will help others decide if this book is for them.

Let me know if this guide has improved you and made you feel excited and energized to approach your dating life.

Thank you so much!
John K. Hunt

SCAN the QR code below

to leave a review on Amazon.

Made in the USA
Coppell, TX
14 April 2023